Phonics PARTY

4

Double Letter Sounds

WorldCom Edu

CONTENTS

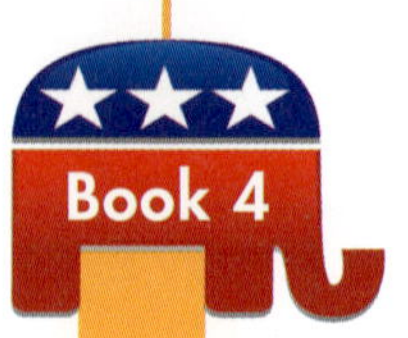

Unit 1	cl	clock / class / clap	4
	gl	glove / glass / glad	
	pl	plane / plate / plant	
	sl	slow / slide / slim	
Unit 2	br	bride / bread / brick	10
	dr	drive / drum / drink	
	fr	frog / frame / front	
	tr	truck / train / trumpet	
Review 1	Double letter consonants 1		16
Unit 3	sk	skunk / skin / skate	22
	sm	small / smoke / smell	
	sn	snack / snail / snow	
	sp	spider / sport / space	
Unit 4	ch	church / cherry / bench	28
	ph	photo / phone / phonics	
	sh	sheep / shirt / fish	
	th	thumb / math / month	
Review 2	Double letter consonants 2		34

Book 4

Unit 5	**ai**	tail / rain / mail	**40**
	ay	pray / play / hay	
	ea	tea / sea / read	
	ee	bee / tree / sleep	
Unit 6	**ar**	car / star / arm	**46**
	or	fork / horse / north	
	er	teacher / soccer / water	
	ir	bird / girl / skirt	
	ur	purple / purse / turtle	
Review 3	**Double letter vowels 1**		**52**
Unit 7	**oa**	boat / road / soap	**58**
	ow 1	yellow / bowl / window	
	ou	mouth / house / count	
	ow 2	cow / owl / bow	
Unit 8	**oi**	point / coin / soil	**64**
	oy	toy / oyster / boy	
	oo 1	book / wood / foot	
	oo 2	food / moon / zoo	
Review 4	**Double letter vowels 2**		**70**
Extra 1	**Y as a vowel**		**76**
Extra 2	**Hard and soft c and g**		**80**

Double letter consonants
cl gl pl sl

PP4-01
MP3

 Listen and repeat. 01 / Unit 1

 c +  l →  cl

clock

class

clap

 g +  l →  gl

glove

glass

glad

Date . . .

 Listen and repeat. MP3 **02** / Unit 1

 p  l → pl

plane

plate

plant

 s  l → sl

slow

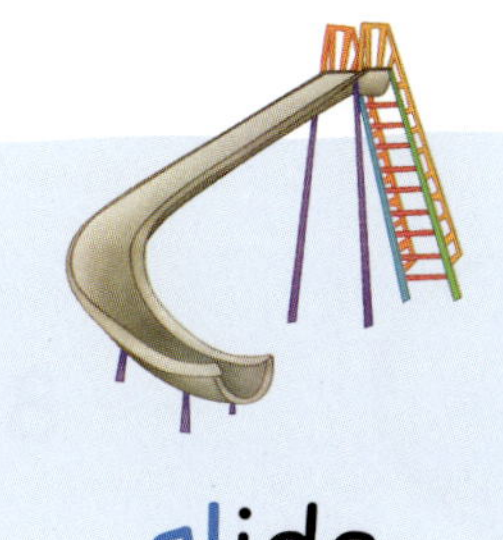

slide

slim

3. Learn

Listen and write the beginning double letters. MP3 **03** / Unit 1

1 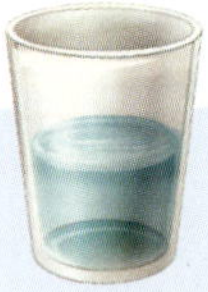 gl

2 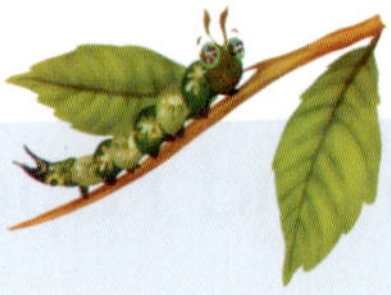

3 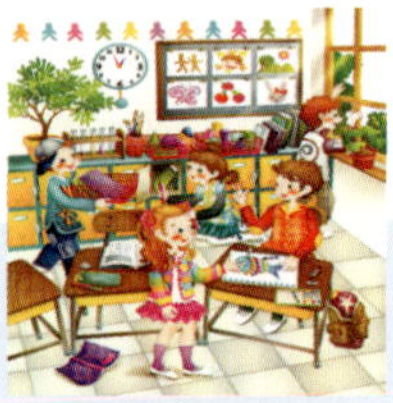

4 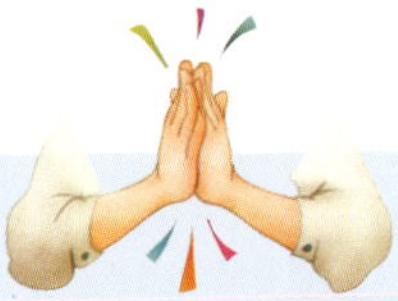

5 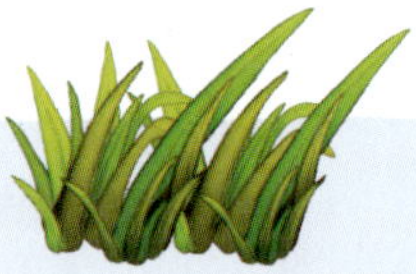

6 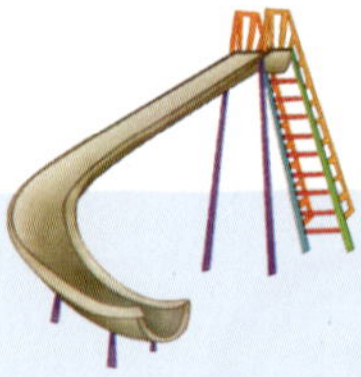

7 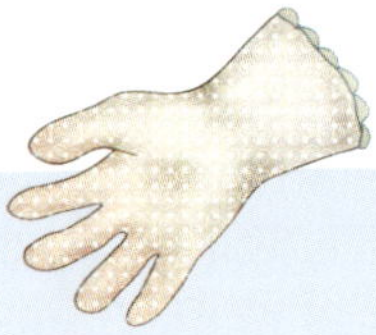

8 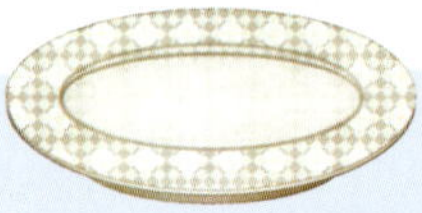

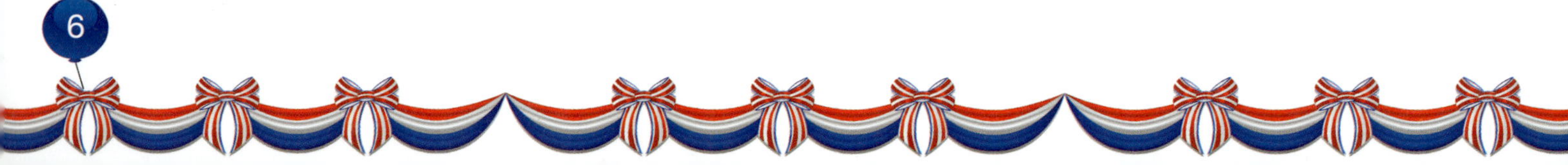

Date   .   .   .

4. Practice

Listen and circle the correct pictures. **MP3** **04** / Unit 1

1 

2 

3 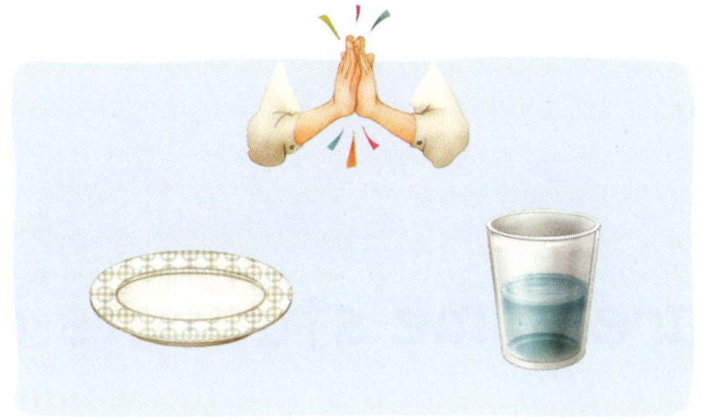

4 

Listen and fill in the blanks. **MP3** **05** / Unit 1

 **cl**ass

 ______ide

 ______ane

 ______ass

Look at the pictures. Fill in the blanks.

glass	class	slide	plane

The <u>plane</u> can fly.

There are some students in the ___________ .

The ___________ is very long.

This is a ___________ of water.

6. Homework

Connect and write the beginning double letters.

Double letter consonants
br   dr   fr   tr

1. Listen

PP4-02
MP3

🎧 Listen and repeat. 📄 **06** / Unit2

b + r → **br**

bride

bread

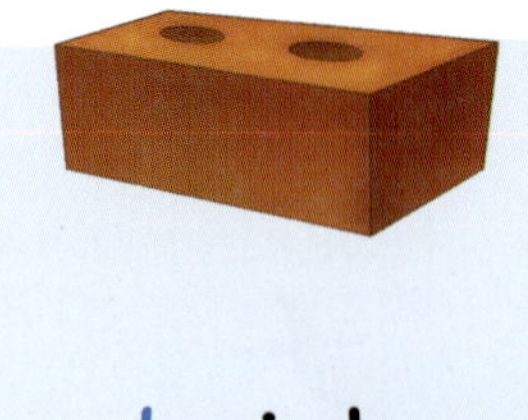

brick

d + r → **dr**

drive

drum

drink

2. Listen

 Listen and repeat.  **07** / Unit 2

 **f** + **r** → **fr**

frog

frame

front

t + **r** → **tr**

  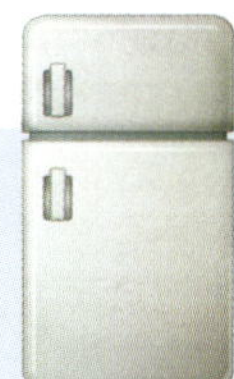

truck

train

trumpet

Listen and write the beginning double letters. MP3 **08** / Unit 2

1

2

3

4

5

6

7

8

Date   .   .   .

4. Practice

🎧 **Listen and circle the correct pictures.** 📄 **09** / Unit 2

1

2

3

4

🎧 **Listen and fill in the blanks.** 📄 **10** / Unit 2

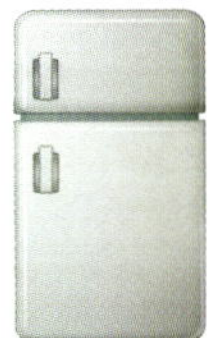 ______ ont

 ______ ain

 ______ ick

 ______ ink

✏️ Look at the pictures. Fill in the blanks.

drink	bride	frog	train

A ___________ has four legs.

The ___________ is beautiful.

People ___________ water every day.

Look at the ___________ .

Date . . .

6. Homework

✏️ Connect and write the beginning double letters.

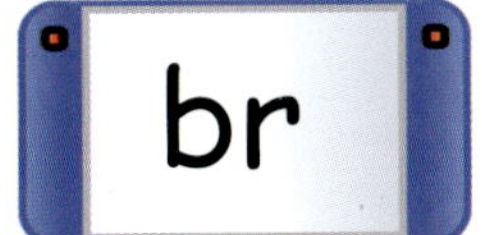

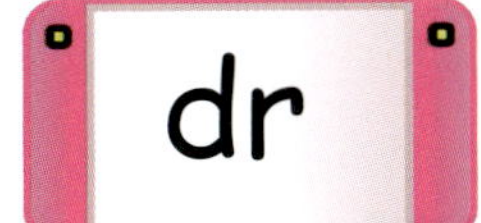

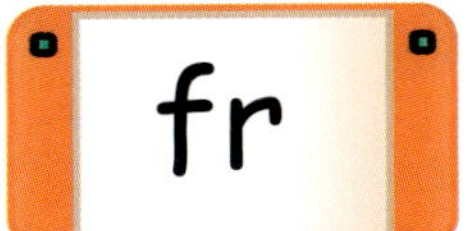

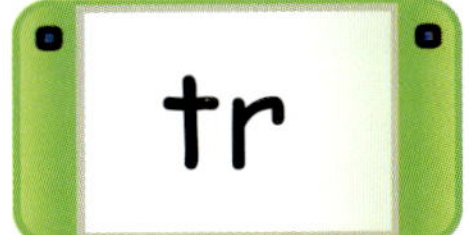

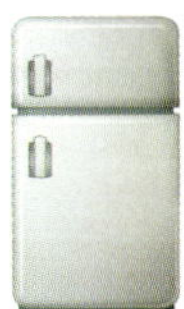

Double letter consonants 1

PP4-R-1
MP3

🎧 Listen and write the numbers. 11 / Review 1

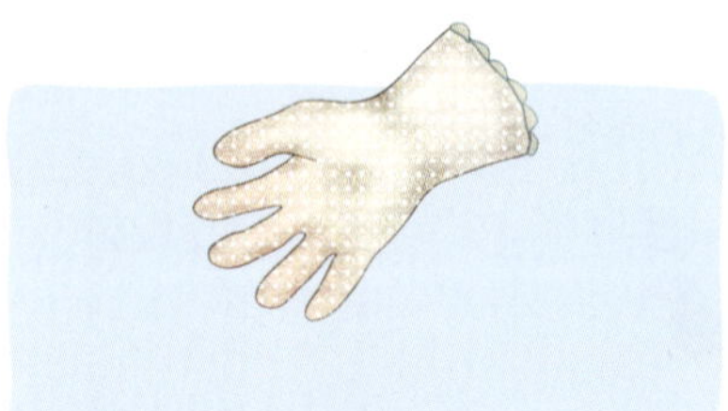

Date . . .

✏️ Find these words on the picture and circle.

✏️ Look and write.

 **Across**

3    6    8 

Down

1    2    4    5    7 

 **Listen and repeat.**  **12** / Review 1

1. The class claps when the clock says 3.

2. She is glad the glove is not glass.

3. A plant eats a plate on a plane.

4. The slim slow snail slides.

5. The bride eats bread in a brick house.

6. I drive with a drum and drink milk.

7. A frog is on the front of the frame.

8. Play the trumpet on the truck or the train.

 Listen and write the words. MP3 **13** / Review 1

1 __________ 6 __________

2 __________ 7 __________

3 __________ 8 __________

4 __________ 9 __________

5 __________ 10 __________

Score __________

Listen and write the sight words. 🎧 **MP3 14** / Review 1

1   every

2   know

3   draw

4   after

✏️ Find the sight words. ↓ → ↘ ↑

every
know
draw
after

a	k	n	o	w
f	a	r	w	k
t	d	v	a	l
e	v	e	r	y
r	j	a	d	t

Double letter consonants

sk sm sn sp

PP4-03
MP3

🎧 Listen and repeat. .MP3 **15** / Unit 3

 **s**  +  **k**  →  **sk**

skunk

skin

skate

 **s**  +  **m**  →  **sm**

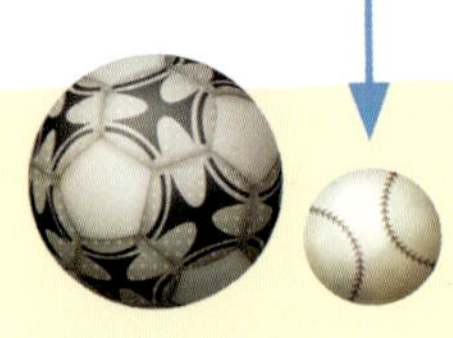

small

smoke

smell

Date　　　.　　　.

2. Listen

 Listen and repeat. **MP3** 16 / Unit 3

s + n → sn

 snack

 snail

 snow

s + p → sp

 spider

 sport

 space

Listen and write the beginning double letters. **MP3 17** / Unit 3

1

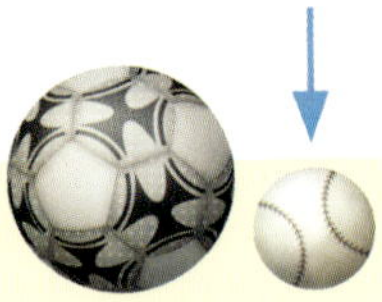

2

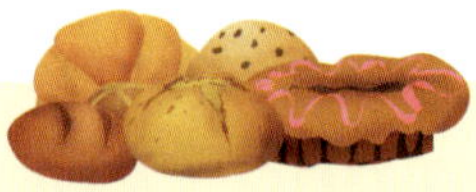

3

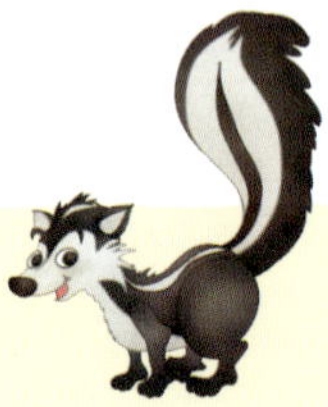

4

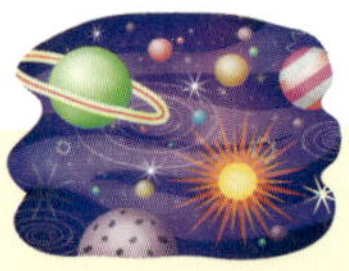

5

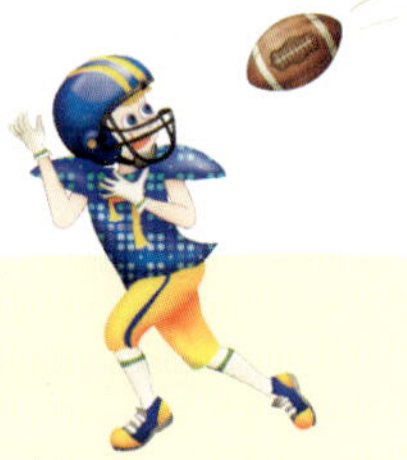

6

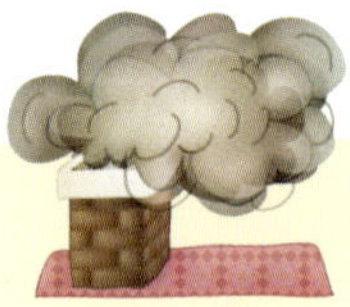

7

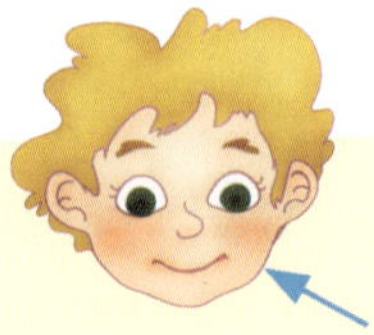

8

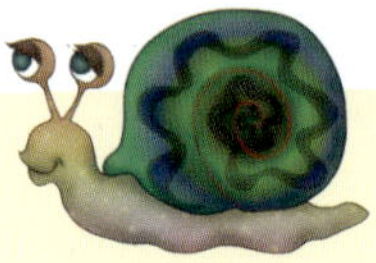

Date ___ . ___ . ___

4. Practice

🎧 **Listen and circle the correct pictures.** 📱 **18** / Unit 3

1 

2 

3 

4 

🎧 **Listen and fill in the blanks.** 📱 **19** / Unit 3

 ______ ate

 ______ oke

 ______ ace

 ______ ack

Look at the pictures. Fill in the blanks.

> snow   skunk   spider   small

The _______ is cold.

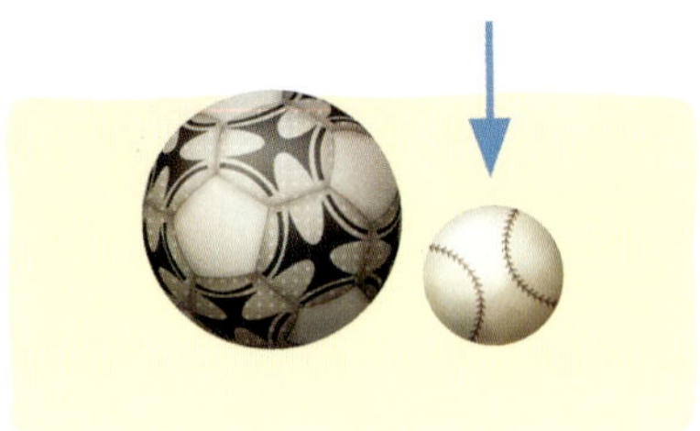

The baseball is _______.

A _______ has eight legs.

The _______ has a long tail.

6. Homework

Date . . .

✏️ Match the pictures that have the same double letters.

✏️ Unscramble the words.

k n s i

skin

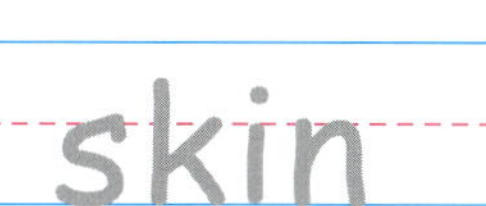

c a p e s

m e l s l

w s o n

Double letter consonants
ch ph sh th

PP4-04
MP3

🎧 Listen and repeat.  **20** / Unit 4

(c) + (h) → **ch**

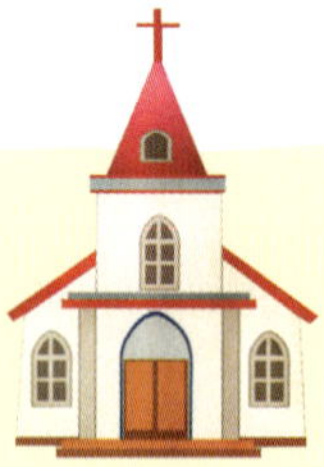

church 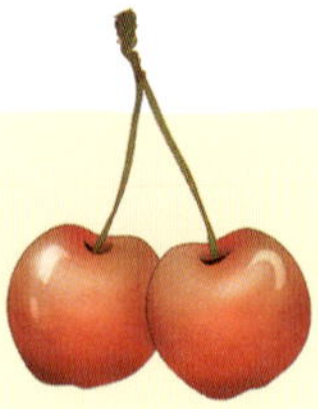   **cherry**   ben**ch**

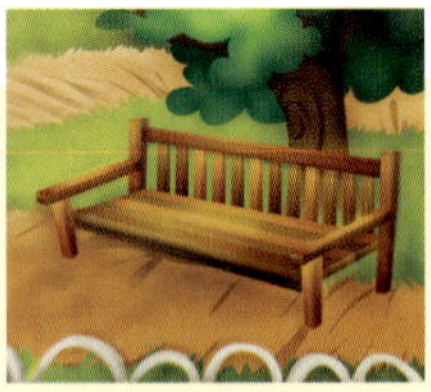

(p) + (h) → **ph**

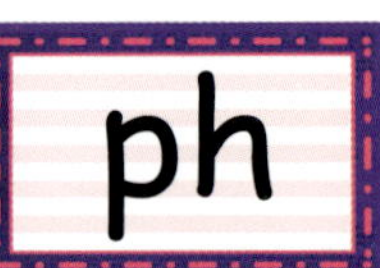

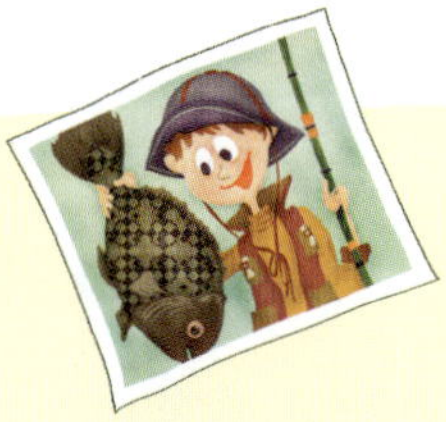

photo   **ph**one   **ph**onics

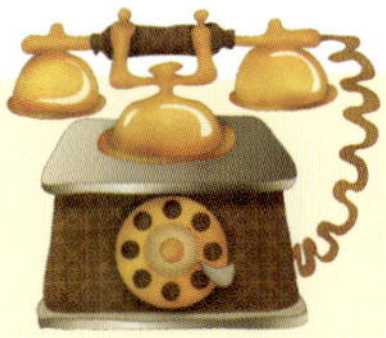

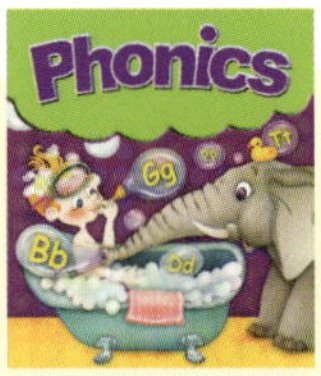

Date　　　.　　　.　　　.

  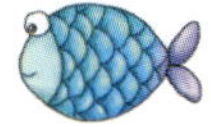    

2. Listen

🎧 Listen and repeat.　📱 **21** / Unit 4

 s　＋　 h　➡　 sh

sheep

shirt

fish

 t　＋　 h　➡　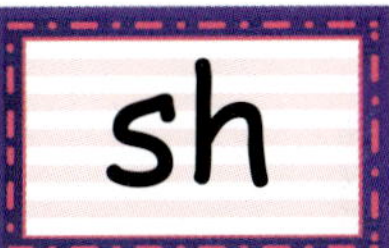 th

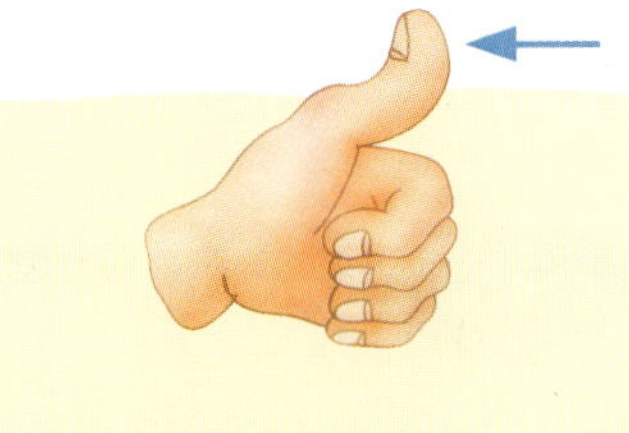

thumb

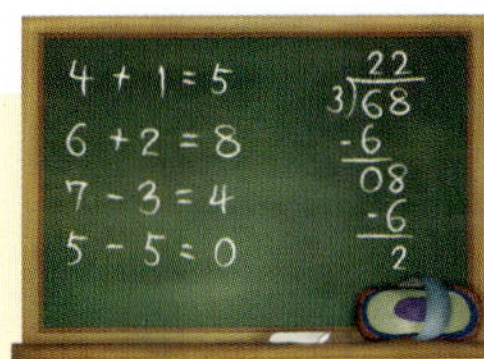

math

month

3. Learn

🎧 Listen and write the beginning or ending double letters. **MP3** **22** / Unit 4

1  

2  

3  

4  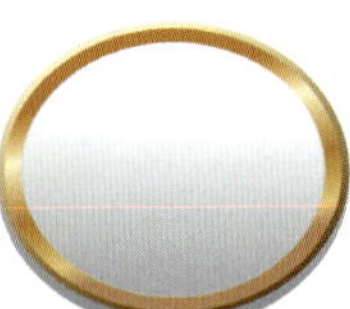

5  

6  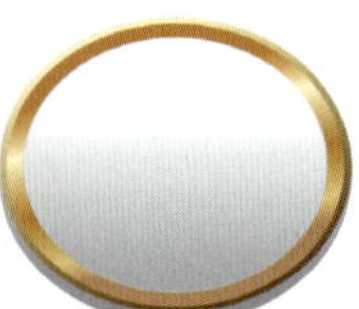

7 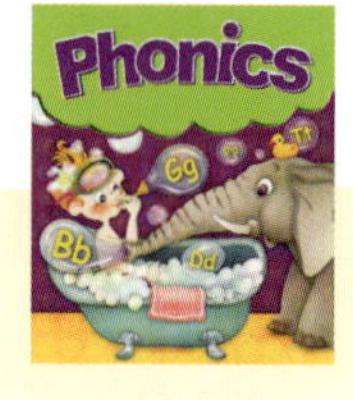 

8  

Date　　　.　　.　　.

4. Practice

 Listen and circle the correct pictures. **23** / Unit 4

1 

2 

3 

4 

 Listen and fill in the blanks. **24** / Unit 4

 _______ one

 fi_______

 _______ urch

 mon_______

Look at the pictures. Fill in the blanks.

church   fish   month   photo

Look at the __________ .

The __________ lives in the water.

There are twelve __________ s in a year.

Many people go to __________ on Sunday.

6. Homework

Date   .   .   .

✏️ **Match the pictures that have the same double letters.**

 •   •  •   • 

 •   • 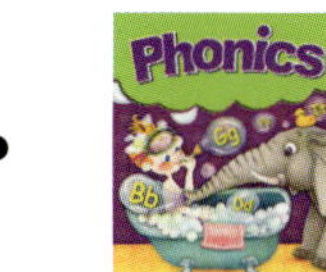 •   • 

 •   • 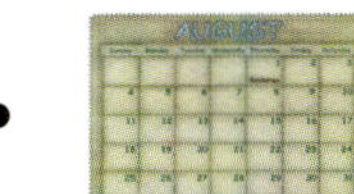 •   • 

 •   •  •   • 

✏️ **Unscramble the words.**

   h o t p o

____

   e p e h s

____

   m t a h

____

   c b n h e

____

Double letter consonants 2

MP3

🎧 Listen and write the numbers.  25 / Review 2

    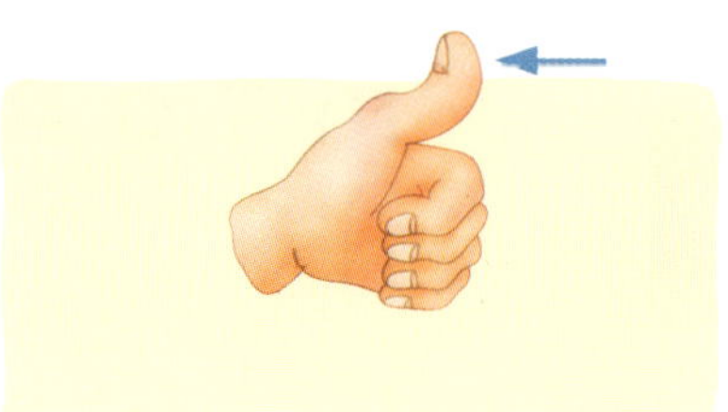 

Date　.　.　.

📝 **Find these words on the picture and circle.**

 Look and write.

Across   **Down**

1    2 

4    3 

6    5 

7    6 

 **Listen and repeat.** **26** / Review 2

1. A skunk on a skate scrapes his skin.

2. I smell smoke from the small pot.

3. A snail eats a snack in the snow.

4. A spider in space plays sports.

5. I see a cherry on a bench in the church.

6. We see a phone and a photo in the phonics book.

7. The sheep and fish have a red shirt.

8. We use our thumb to do math every month.

 Listen and write the words.  **27** / Review 2

1 __________   6 __________

2 __________   7 __________

3 __________   8 __________

4 __________   9 __________

5 __________   10 __________

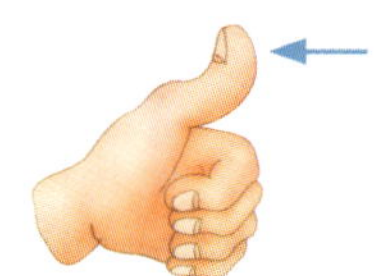

Score __________

Sight words

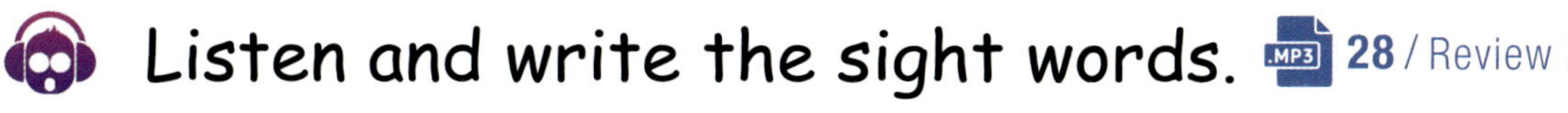 Listen and write the sight words. **.MP3** **28** / Review 2

1 shoe

2 their

3 she

4 shall

 Find the sight words. ↓ → ↘ ↑

shoe	
their	
she	
shall	

s	n	t	l	r
h	h	w	g	i
a	e	o	i	e
l	s	h	e	h
l	h	e	n	t

Double letter vowels
ai ay ea ee

🎧 Listen and repeat.  **29** / Unit 5

a + i → ai

tail

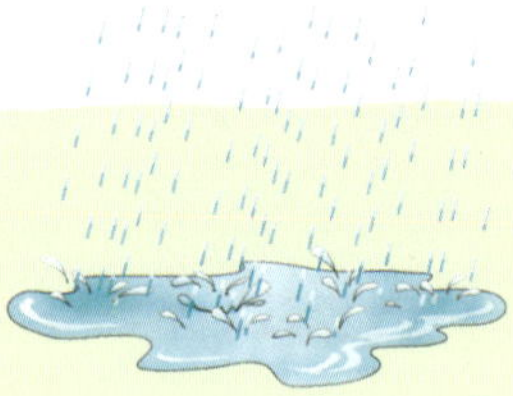

rain

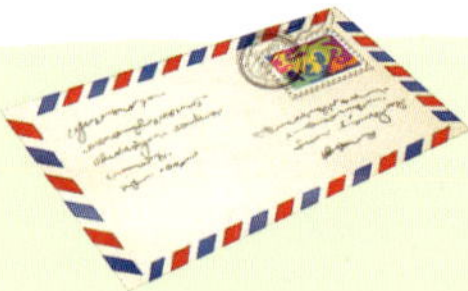

mail

a + y → ay

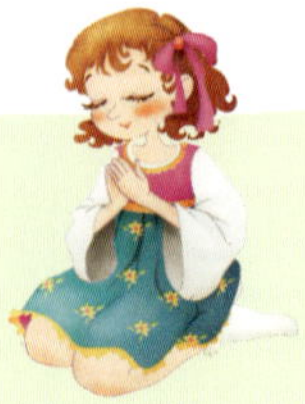

pray

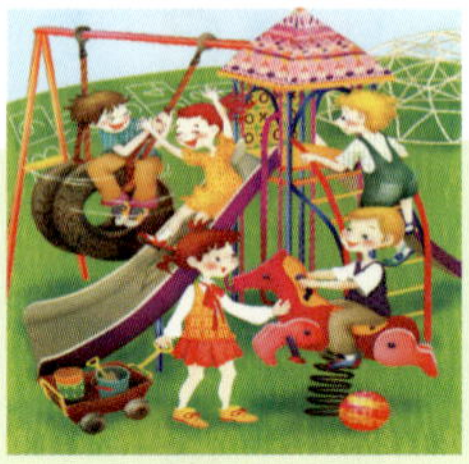

play

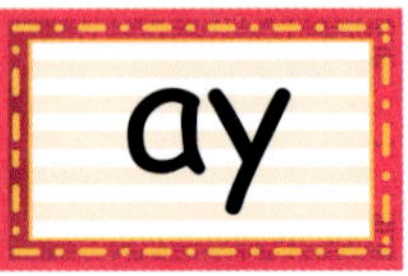

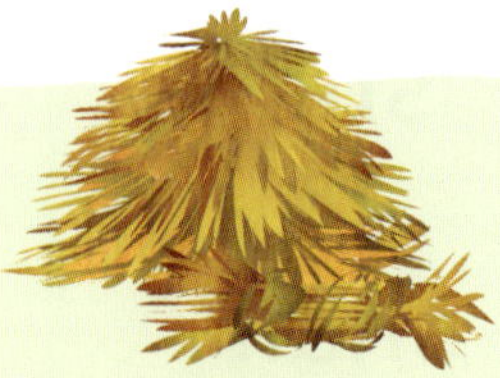

hay

Date   .   .   .

  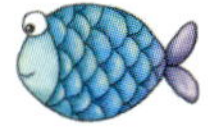    

2. Listen

 Listen and repeat. **30** / Unit 5

e + a → ea

tea

sea

read

e + e → ee

bee

tree

sleep

 Listen and write the words correctly. MP3 **31** / Unit 5

1  trea

tree

2  reed

3  mayl

4  plai

5  tee

6  tayl

7  sleap

8  hai

Date . . .

4. Practice

Listen and circle the correct pictures. 📱 **32** / Unit 5

1 

2 

3 

4 

Listen and fill in the blanks. 📱 **33** / Unit 5

 m ____ l

 tr ____

 r ___ d

 pr ____

Look at the pictures. Fill in the blanks.

tree	mail	play	sea

The _________ is tall.

We like to _________.

Here is the _________.

I want to go to the _________.

Date   .   .   .

6. Homework

 Circle the correct double letters.

Double letter vowels
ar or er ir ur

PP4-06
MP3

🎧 Listen and repeat.  **34** / Unit 6

 **a** +  **r** ➡ **ar**

car

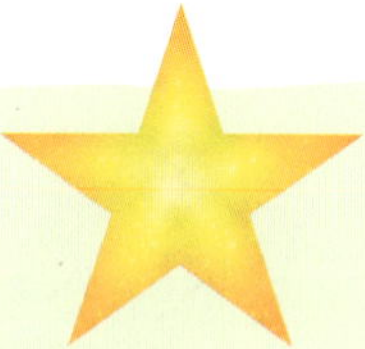

star

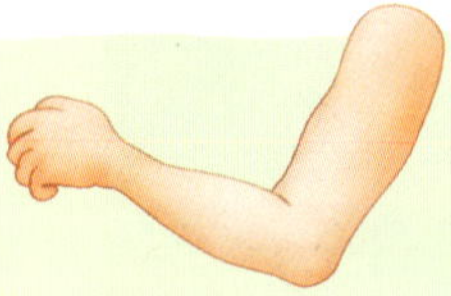

arm

 **o** + 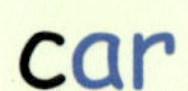 **r** ➡ **or**

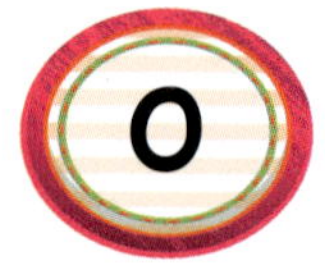

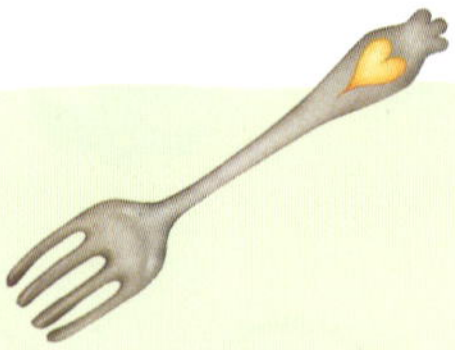

fork

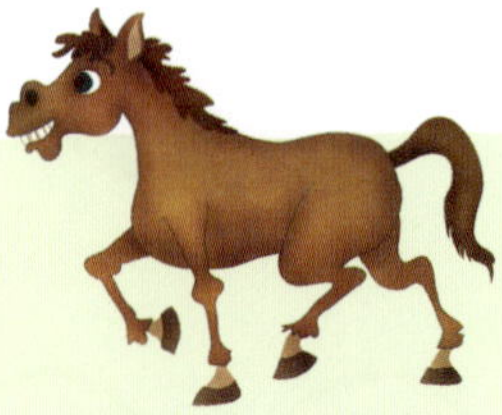

horse

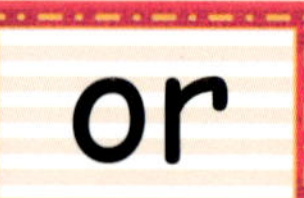

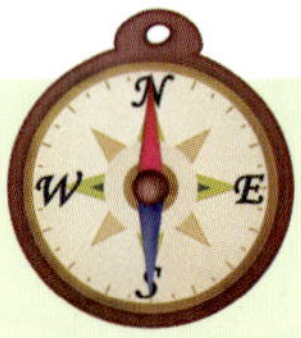

north

2. Listen

Date . . .

🎧 Listen and repeat. MP3 **35** / Unit 6

| e | + | r | → | er |

teacher  | soccer  | water

| i | + | r | → | ir |

bird  | girl  | skirt

| u | + | r | → | ur |

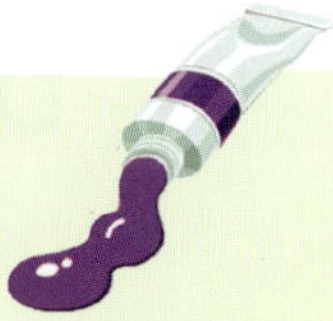

purple  | purse  | turtle

3. Learn

 Listen and write the words correctly. **36** / Unit 6

1 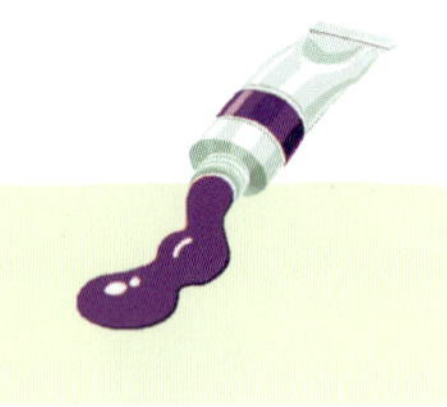 perple
____

2  soccar
____

3  cor
____

4  skurt
____

5  fark
____

6  tirtle
____

7  watur
____

8  berd
____

Date ___ . ___ . ___ .

4. Practice

Listen and circle the correct pictures. 🎧 **MP3** **37** / Unit 6

1 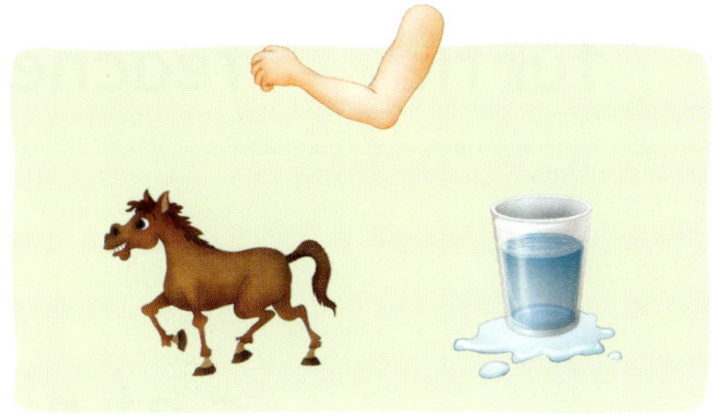

2 

3 

4 

Listen and fill in the blanks. 🎧 **MP3** **38** / Unit 6

 g____l

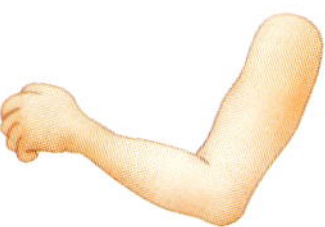 ____m

 n____th

 p____se

✏️ Look at the pictures. Fill in the blanks.

> horse   star   bird   turtle   teacher

We see __________ s at night.

The __________ is too slow.

A __________ has wings.

She is a __________ .

Do you want to ride a __________ ?

Date   .   .   .

6. Homework

Circle the correct double letters.

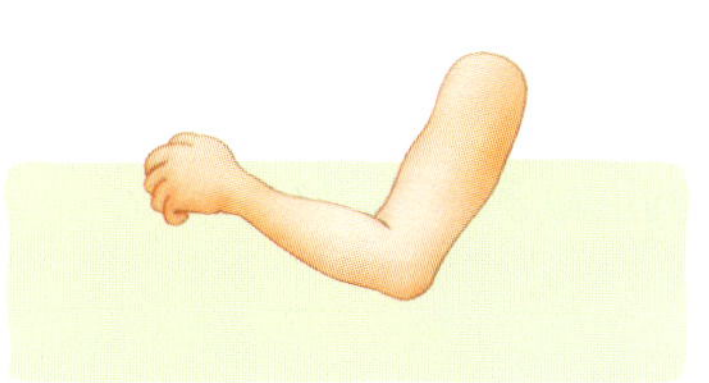

 ar    er

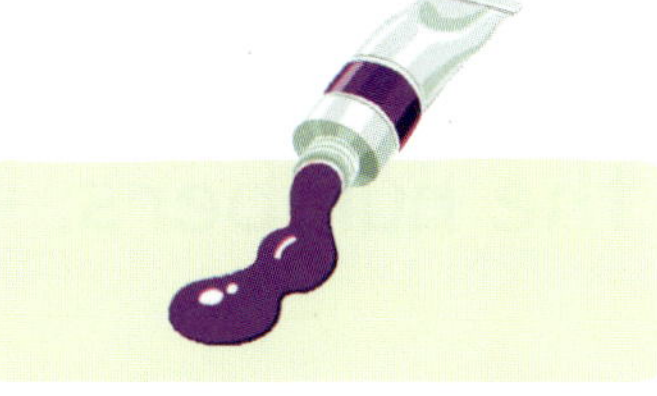

 ir    ur

 or    er

 ir    ur

 ar    or

 ir    ur

 ar    er

 ir    ur

 or    er

Double letter vowels 1

MP3

🎧 Listen and write the numbers. 📄 39 / Review 3

Date . . .

✏️ **Find these words on the picture and circle.**

Double letters

✏️ Look and write.

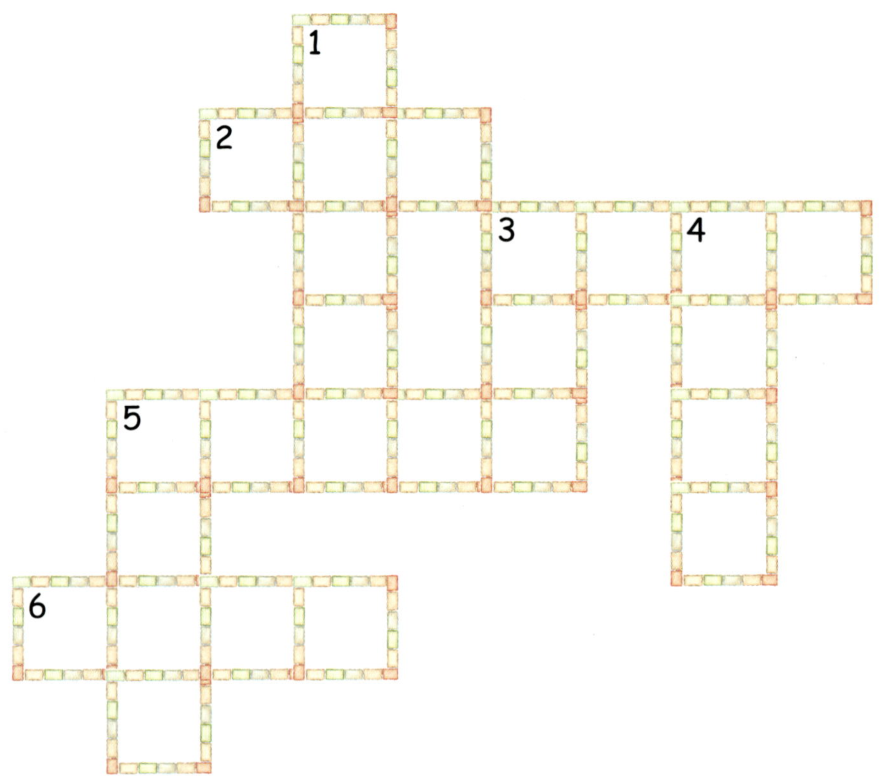

Across

2  3  5  6 

Down

1  3  4  5 

 Listen and repeat.  **40** / Review 3

1. I mail a toy tail in the rain.

2. We play and pray on the hay.

3. I read by the sea and drink tea.

4. The bee sleeps in a tree.

5. The star on the car has one arm.

6. A horse runs north with a big fork.

7. My teacher plays soccer and drinks water.

8. The girl with the skirt sings like a bird.

9. Your turtle has a purple purse.

Listen and write the words.  **41** / Review 3

1 __________   6 __________

2 __________   7 __________

3 __________   8 __________

4 __________   9 __________

5 __________   10 __________

Score __________

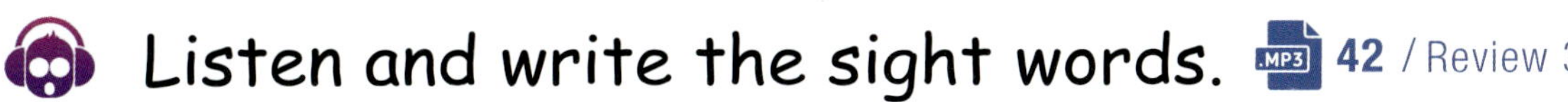

Listen and write the sight words. **.MP3 42** / Review 3

1 said

2 better

3 around

4 carry

Find the sight words. ↓ → ↘ ↑

said	better	around	carry

b	s	a	i	d
e	r	s	c	n
t	e	i	a	u
t	t	a	r	o
e	e	d	r	r
r	b	r	y	a

Double letter vowels

oa ow 1 ou ow 2

PP4-07
MP3

Listen and repeat. **43** / Unit 7

o + a → oa

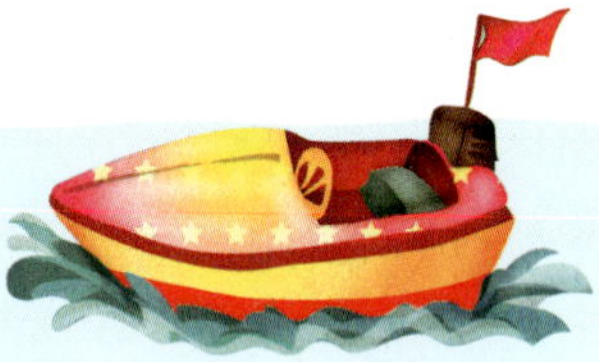

b**oa**t

r**oa**d

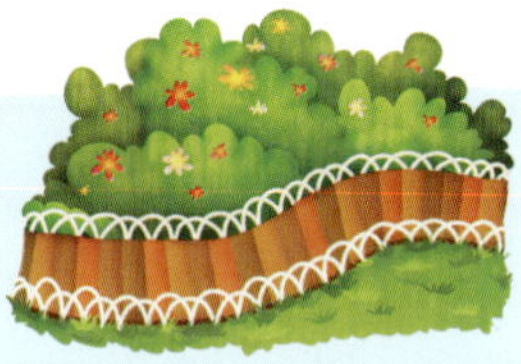

s**oa**p

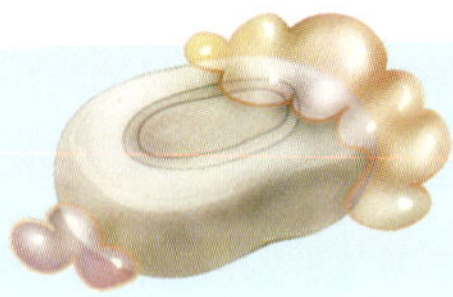

45 / Unit 8

o + w → ow

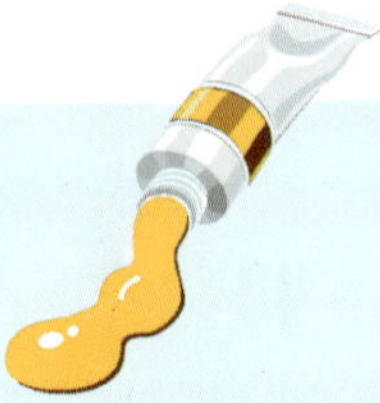

yell**ow**

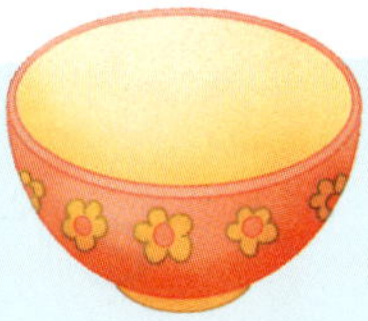

b**ow**l

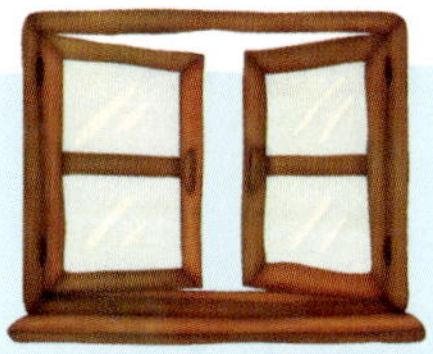

wind**ow**

Date   .   .   .

2. Listen

 Listen and repeat.   **44** / Unit 7

o + u → **ou**

mouth

house

count

o + w → **ow**

cow

owl

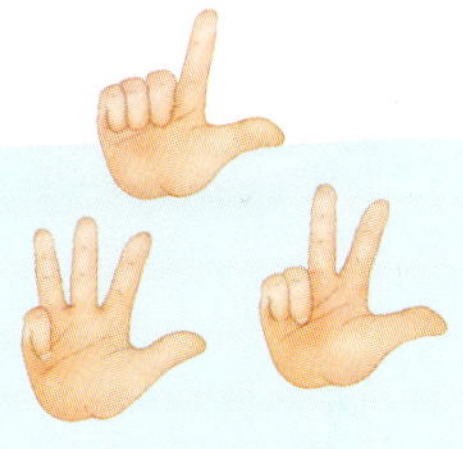

bow

59

 Listen and write the words correctly. .MP3 **45** / Unit 7

1  boul
____

2  sowp
____

3  bout
____

4 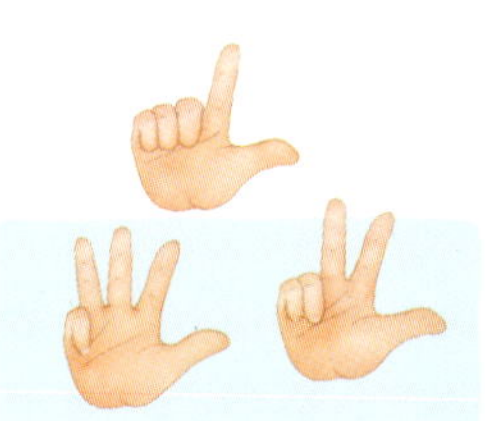 coant
____

5  windou
____

6  cou
____

7  howse
____

8 oal
____

Date　　.　　.　　.

4. Practice

🎧 **Listen and circle the correct pictures.** 🎵 **46** / Unit 7

1 

2 

3 

4 

🎧 **Listen and fill in the blanks.** 🎵 **47** / Unit 7

 h____se

 r____d

 ____l

 yell____

Look at the pictures. Fill in the blanks.

house   window   Cow   boat

Can you close the _______?

This is my _______.

There is a _______.

_______s make milk.

Date ____ . ____ . ____

6. Homework

✏️ **Match the pictures to the correct double letters.**

1  • • oa • • 

 • • ow • • 

2  • • ou • • 

 • • ow • •

✏️ **Unscramble the words.**

 o b w

____

 s a p o

____

 b l w o

____

 n c u t o

____

UNIT 8

Double letter vowels

oi oy oo1 oo2

 Listen and repeat.  **48** / Unit 8

 o  + i  → oi

point

coin

soil

 o  + y  → oy

toy

oyster

boy

Date　　.　　.　　.

2. Listen

 Listen and repeat.  **49** / Unit 8

o + o → oo

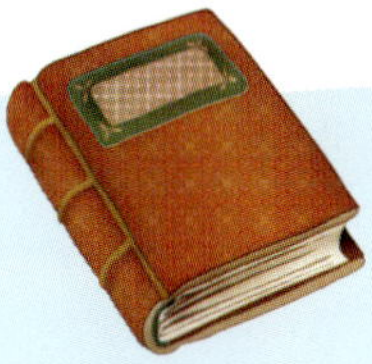

book 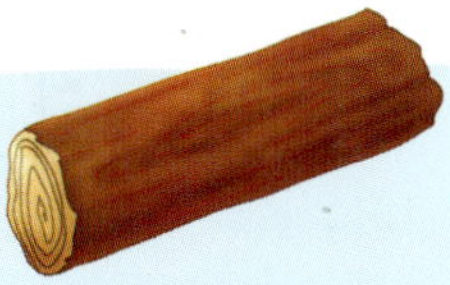　　　　wood 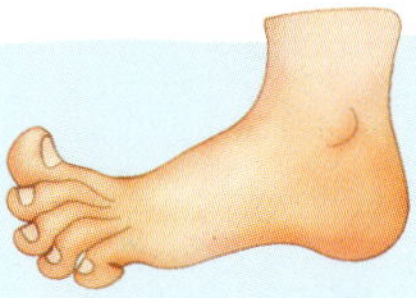　　　　foot

o + o → oo

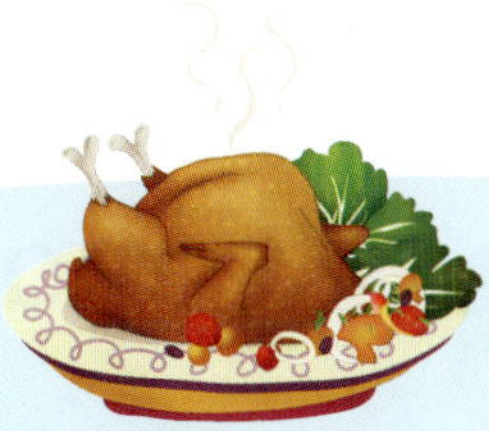

food 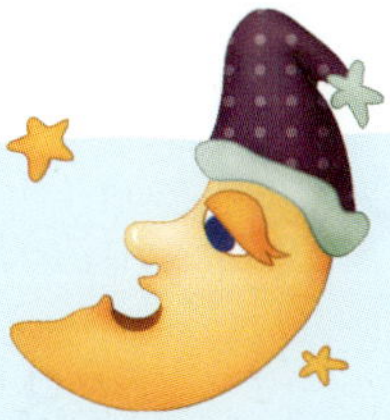　　　　moon 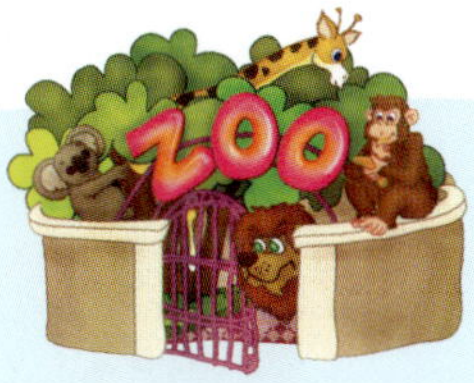　　　　zoo

 Listen and write the words correctly. MP3 **50** / Unit 8

1  oister

2  poont

3  woid

4  soyl

5  boo

6  zoy

7  boyk

8 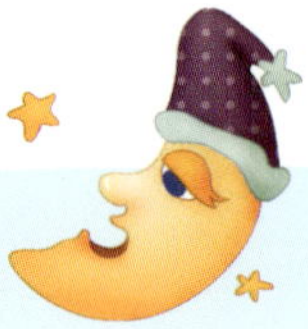  moin

Date   .   .   .

4. Practice

🎧 **Listen and circle the correct pictures.** 🔊 **51** / Unit 8

1 

2 

3 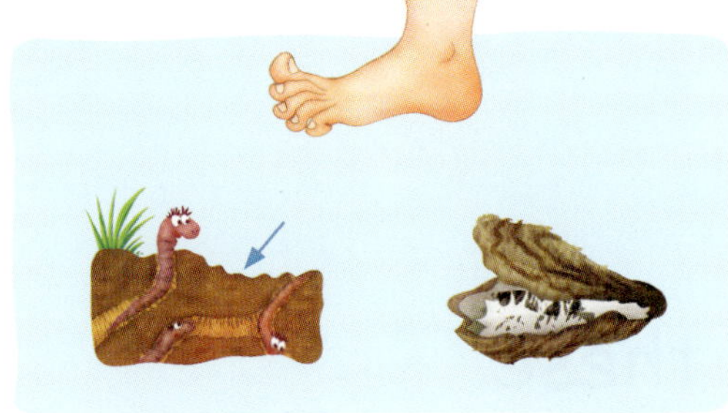

4 

🎧 **Listen and fill in the blanks.** 🔊 **52** / Unit 8

 c _____ n

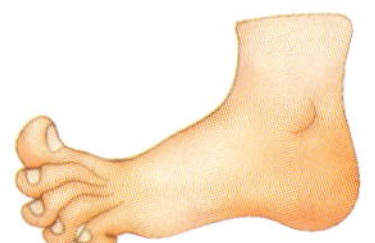 f _____ t

 z _____

 _____ ster

Look at the pictures. Fill in the blanks.

| toy | zoo | foot | coin |

I like ___________ s.

Look at these ___________ s.

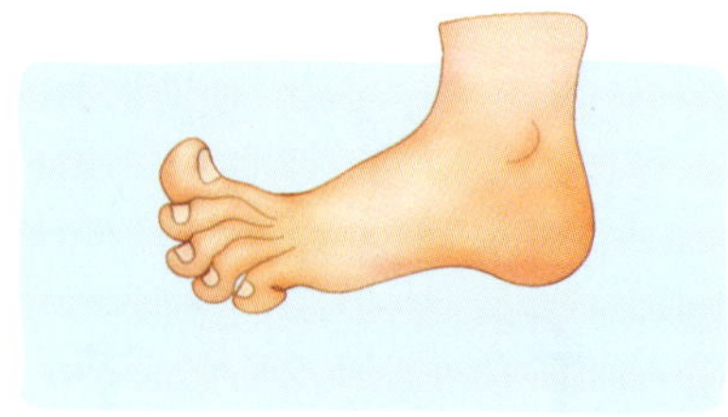

My ___________ is very big.

The animals are in a ___________ .

Date . . .

6. Homework

✏️ **Match the pictures to the correct double letters.**

1  •   • oi •   • 

 •   • oo •   • 

2  •   • oy •   • 

•   • oo •   •

✏️ **Unscramble the words.**

 i c n o

 o d o f

 k o b o

 o t y

Double letter vowels 2

PP4-R-4
MP3

Listen and write the numbers. **MP3** 53 / Review 4

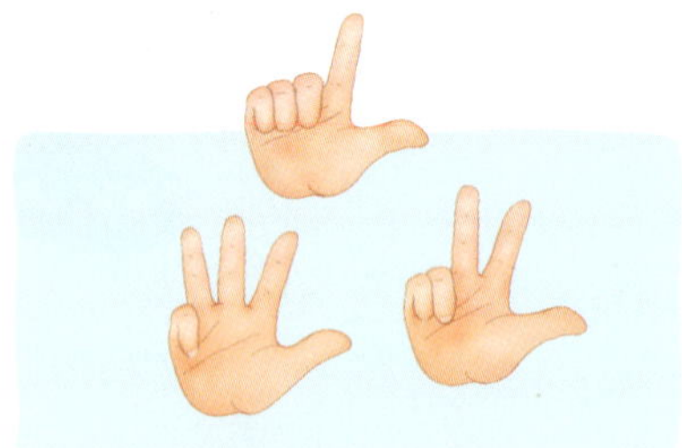 

Double letters

✏ **Find these words on the picture and circle.**

 Look and write.

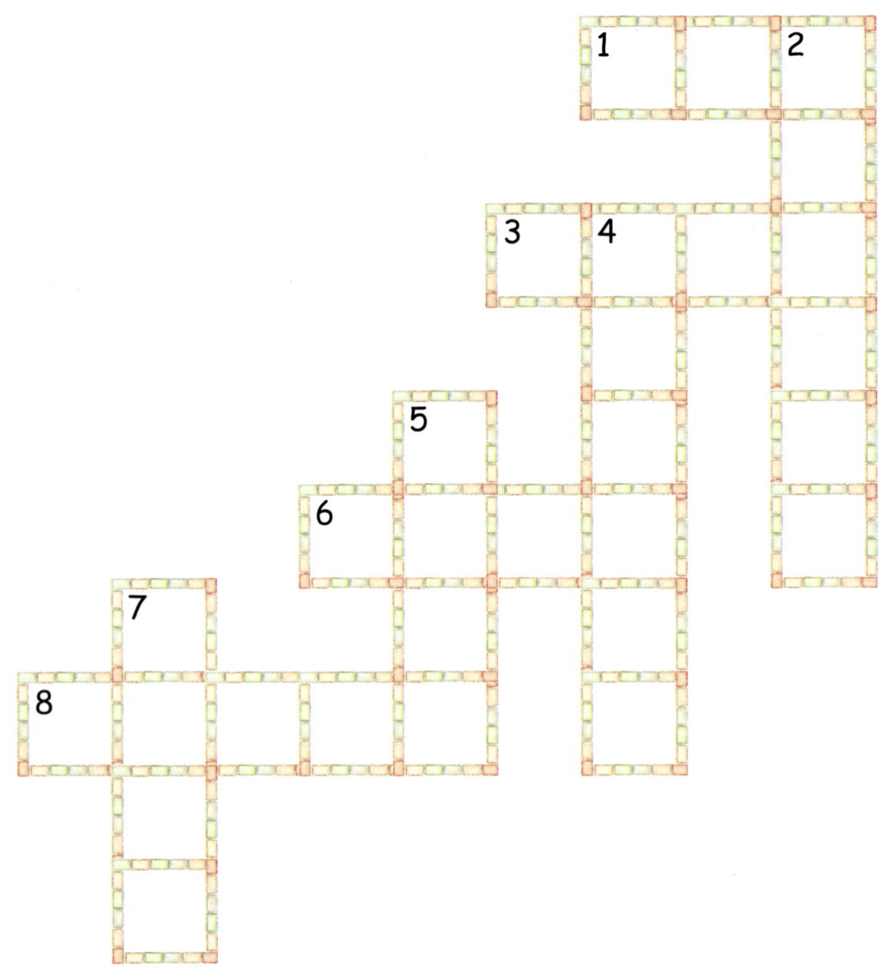

Across

1  3  6  8 

Down

2  4  5  7 

 **Listen and repeat.** MP3 **54** / Review 4

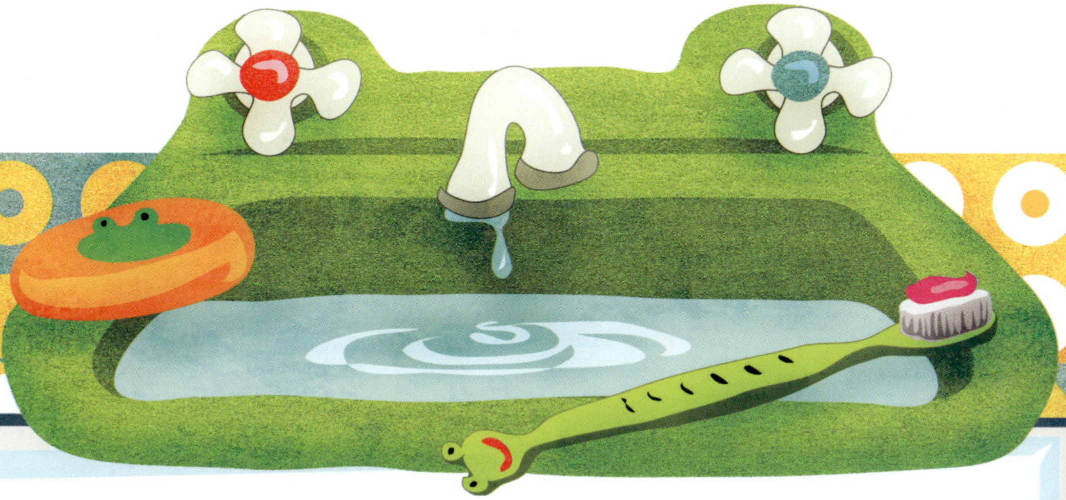

1. The boat with the soap is on the road.

2. I see a yellow bowl near the window.

3. We use our mouth to count the cats in the house.

4. An owl and a cow both bow.

5. He points to the coin in the soil.

6. A boy and an oyster play with the toy.

7. The book has a man with a foot made of wood.

8. We eat food at the zoo on the moon.

 Listen and write the words.  **55** / Review 4

1 __________   6 __________

2 __________   7 __________

3 __________   8 __________

4 __________   9 __________

5 __________   10 __________

Score __________

Sight words

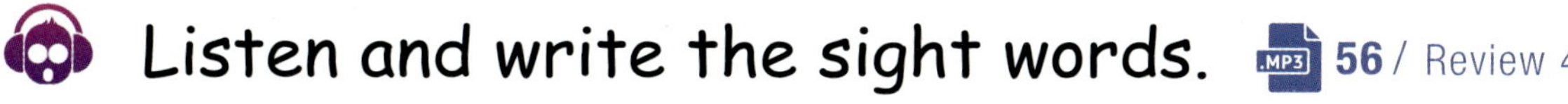

🎧 **Listen and write the sight words.** 📻 **56** / Review 4

1 work

2 found

3 could

4 too

✏️ **Find the sight words.** ↓ → ↘ ↑

work
found
could
too

m	a	f	t	g
n	w	o	r	k
c	o	u	l	d
h	o	n	q	j
d	t	d	s	r

Y as a vowel

PP4-E-1
MP3

🎧 Listen, repeat, and write. .MP3 **57** / Extra 1

y **1 syllable** (long **i** sound)

sky

cry

fly

dry

y **2 syllables** (long **e** sound)

bunny

happy

sunny

baby

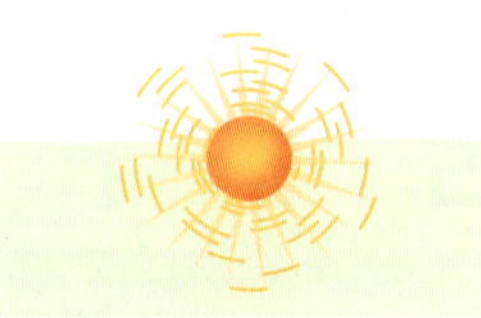

Date . . .

🎧 **Listen and write the words in the correct column.** 📄 **58**/Extra 1

by	windy	pretty	dry
spy	sleepy	fly	study
many	happy	city	shy
funny	why	my	cry

long i sound

sky

long e sound

baby

Look at the pictures. Fill in the blanks.

sunny   sky   bunny   fly

The __________ is very cute.

The __________ is blue.

It is a __________ day.

The __________ can fly.

4. Activity

✏️ **Find these words on the picture and circle.**

Hard and soft c and g

PP4-E-2
MP3

 Listen and repeat. 59 / Extra 2

Hard c (c + a, o, u)	 cat	 cup	 cone
Soft c (c + e, i, y)	 cereal	 city	 cycle
Hard g (g + a, o, u)	 game	 goat	 gum
Soft g (g + e, i, y)	 gentle	 giraffe	 gym

2. Learn

 Listen and write the words in the correct column. .MP3 **60** / Extra 2

cereal	car	cup	lace
coin	cyber	circus	cap
gentle	giraffe	gum	gym
game	golf	giant	gate

hard c sound

soft c sound

hard g sound

soft g sound

✏️ Look at the pictures. Fill in the blanks.

city	cat	game	gentle

I live in the ___________.

The ___________ is fun.

This is my ___________.

This man is very ___________.

4. Activity

✏️ **Find these words on the picture and circle.**

Memo

Phonics PARTY

4

Double Letter Sounds

Workbook

WorldCom Edu

Phonics PARTY

4

Workbook

cl gl pl sl

 Fill in the blanks.

glad

_____ass

_____ock

_____ide

_____ane

_____ant

_____ass

_____ow

B Circle the correct words.

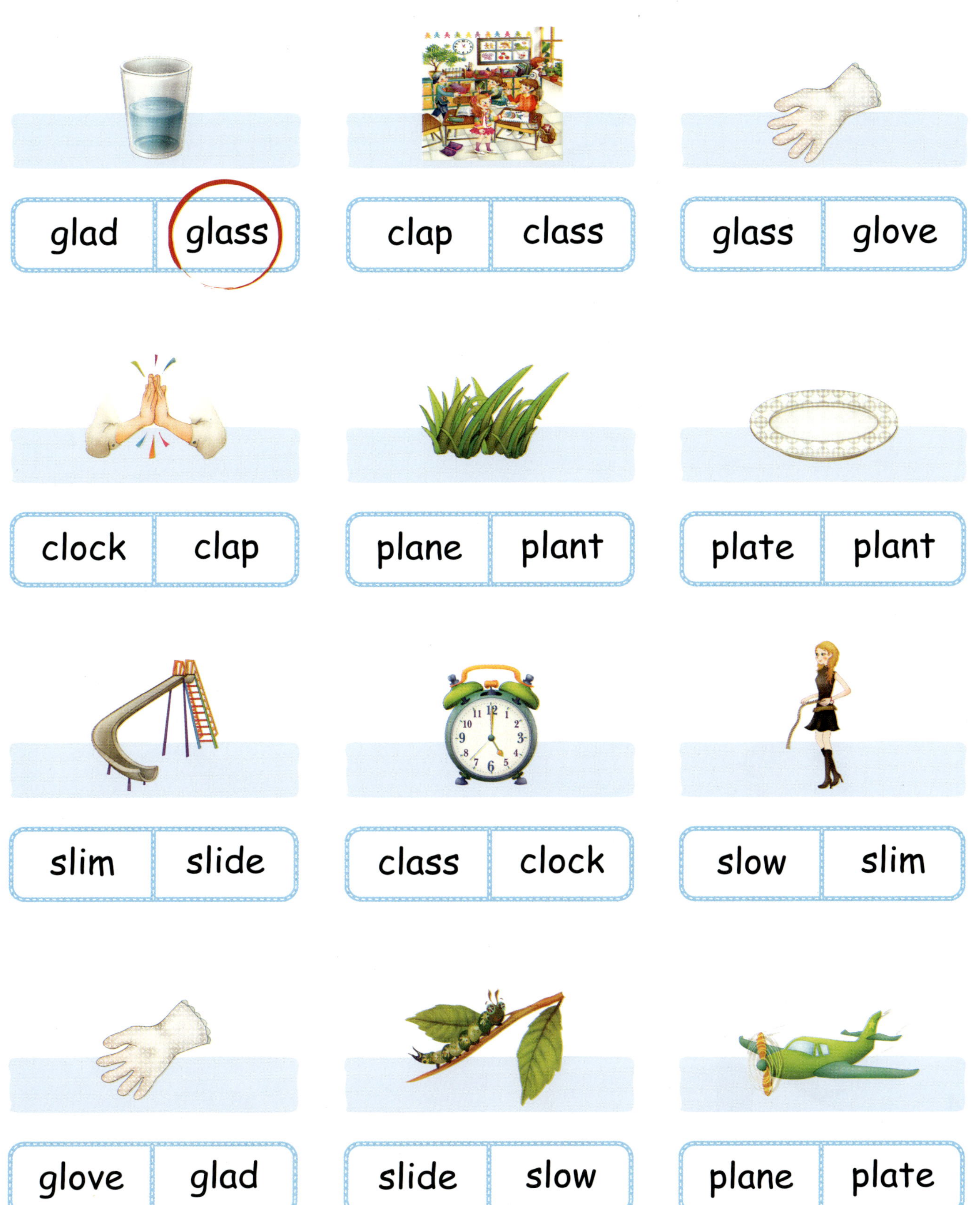

Write the words with the same double letters.

plate	glass	clap	slim
glove	slide	plant	class

1 

clock

_______________ _______________

2 

plane

_______________ _______________

3 

glad

_______________ _______________

4 

slow

_______________ _______________

D Find the words. ↓ → ↘ ↑

clap	plane	slim	glove

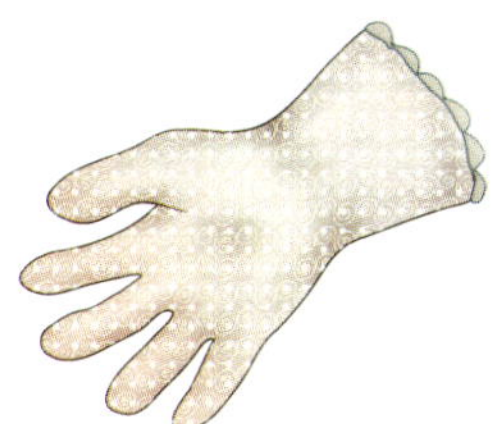

p	l	a	n	e	s
g	p	a	h	t	m
l	c	r	p	c	i
o	u	l	v	f	l
v	g	e	a	l	s
e	s	j	d	p	q

br dr fr tr

A Fill in the blanks.

______ uck

______ ive

______ ick

______ ink

______ ead

______ og

______ ont

______ ain

B Circle the correct words.

 Write the words with the same double letters.

drive   frog   truck   brick

front   bread   drink   trumpet

1 

frame

2 

drum

3 

train

4 

bride

D Find the words. ↓ → ↘ ↑

train   bride   frog   drive

f	d	j	a	m	g
t	l	r	s	n	o
r	c	a	i	x	r
a	t	q	n	v	f
i	b	r	i	d	e
n	l	s	y	l	v

sk   sm   sn   sp

A Fill in the blanks.

___ ow

___ ell

___ in

___ ack

___ ate

___ ace

___ ort

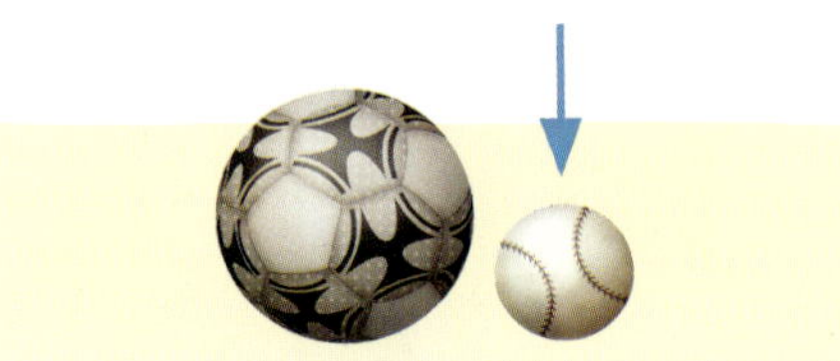

___ all

B Circle the correct words.

c **Write the words with the same double letters.**

| smell | spider | skate | snow |
| snack | skunk | small | space |

1 skin

2 snail

3 sport

4 smoke

D Find the words. ↓ → ↘ ↑

small   sport   skunk   snow

s	m	a	l	l	k
e	s	n	a	l	n
s	r	p	t	s	u
n	u	c	o	v	k
o	s	p	k	r	s
w	n	s	o	b	t

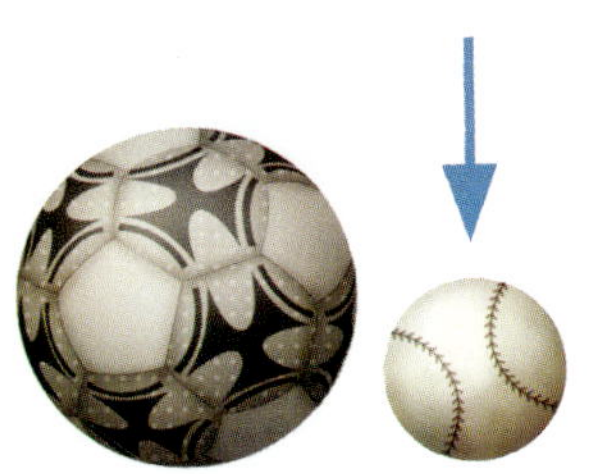

ch ph sh th

 **A** Fill in the blanks.

mon______

ben______

______eep

______oto

______urch

______one

fi______

ma______

B Circle the correct words.

 Write the words with the same double letters.

fish	cherry	month	photo
church	phonics	sheep	thumb

1 shirt

2 bench

3 phone

4 math

D Find the words. ↓ → ↘ ↑

phone   fish   bench   month

f	p	h	o	n	e
h	b	h	y	u	i
t	m	e	a	b	f
n	o	j	n	f	i
o	u	c	s	c	s
m	s	l	t	r	h

UNIT 5

ai ay ea ee

Fill in the blanks.

r _ _ _ d

b _ _ _

m _ _ _ l

pl _ _ _ _

r _ _ _ n

s _ _ _ _

pr _ _ _ _

tr _ _ _

B Circle the correct words.

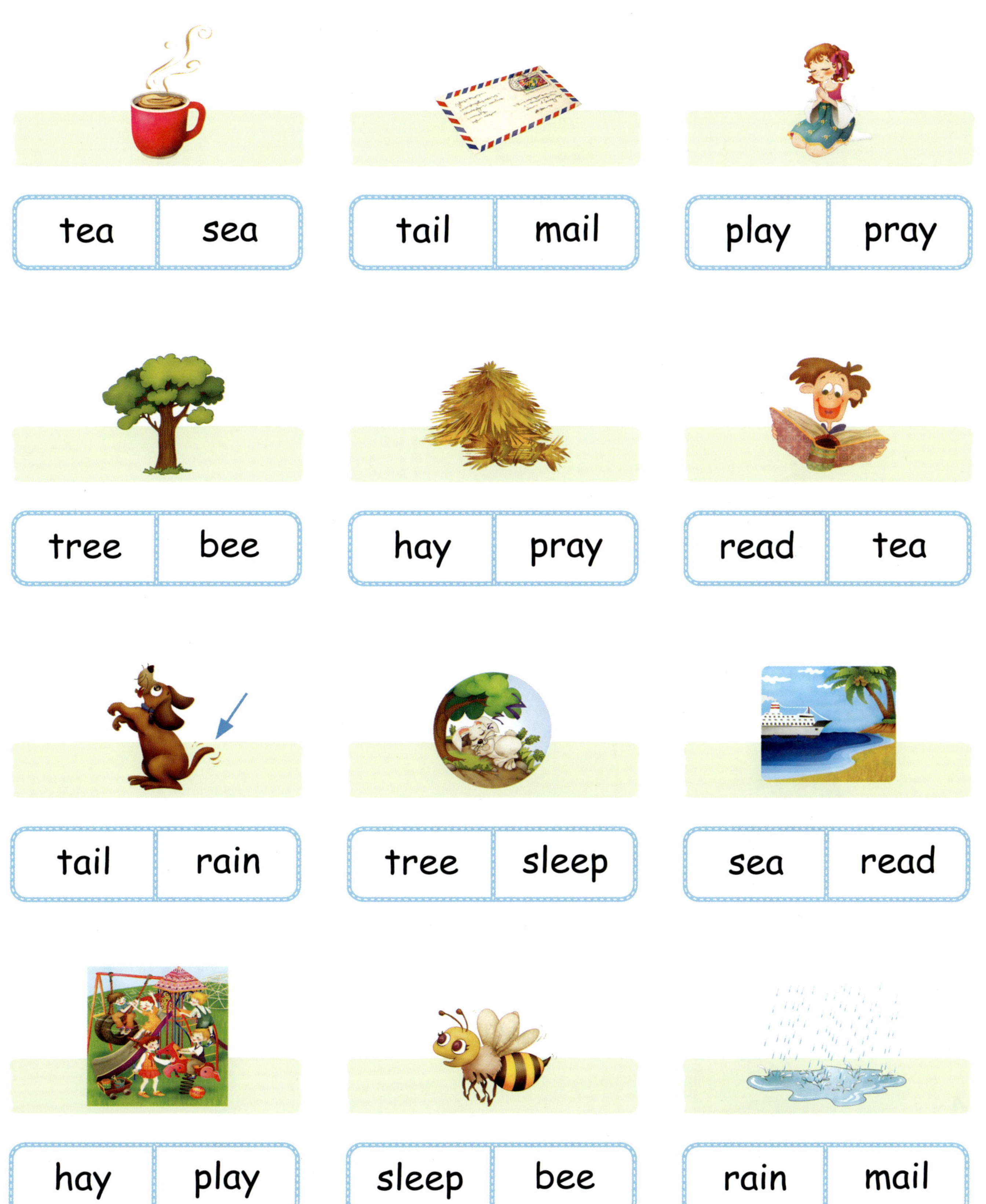

Write the words with the same double letters.

tea	mail	hay	tree
rain	sea	bee	play

1 

pray

_______________   _______________

2 

tail

_______________   _______________

3 

sleep

_______________   _______________

4 

read

_______________   _______________

D Find the words. ↓ → ↘ ↑

sea play sleep mail

l	m	a	l	i	n
i	u	v	d	e	p
a	s	i	z	b	l
m	d	e	e	r	a
j	a	y	a	r	y
a	s	l	e	e	p

ar or er ir ur

A **Fill in the blanks.**

p___se

socc___

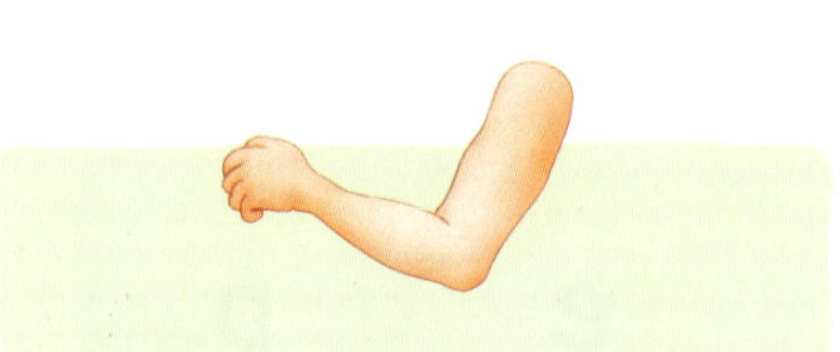

___m

h___se

b___d

c___

t___tle

f___k

B Circle the correct words.

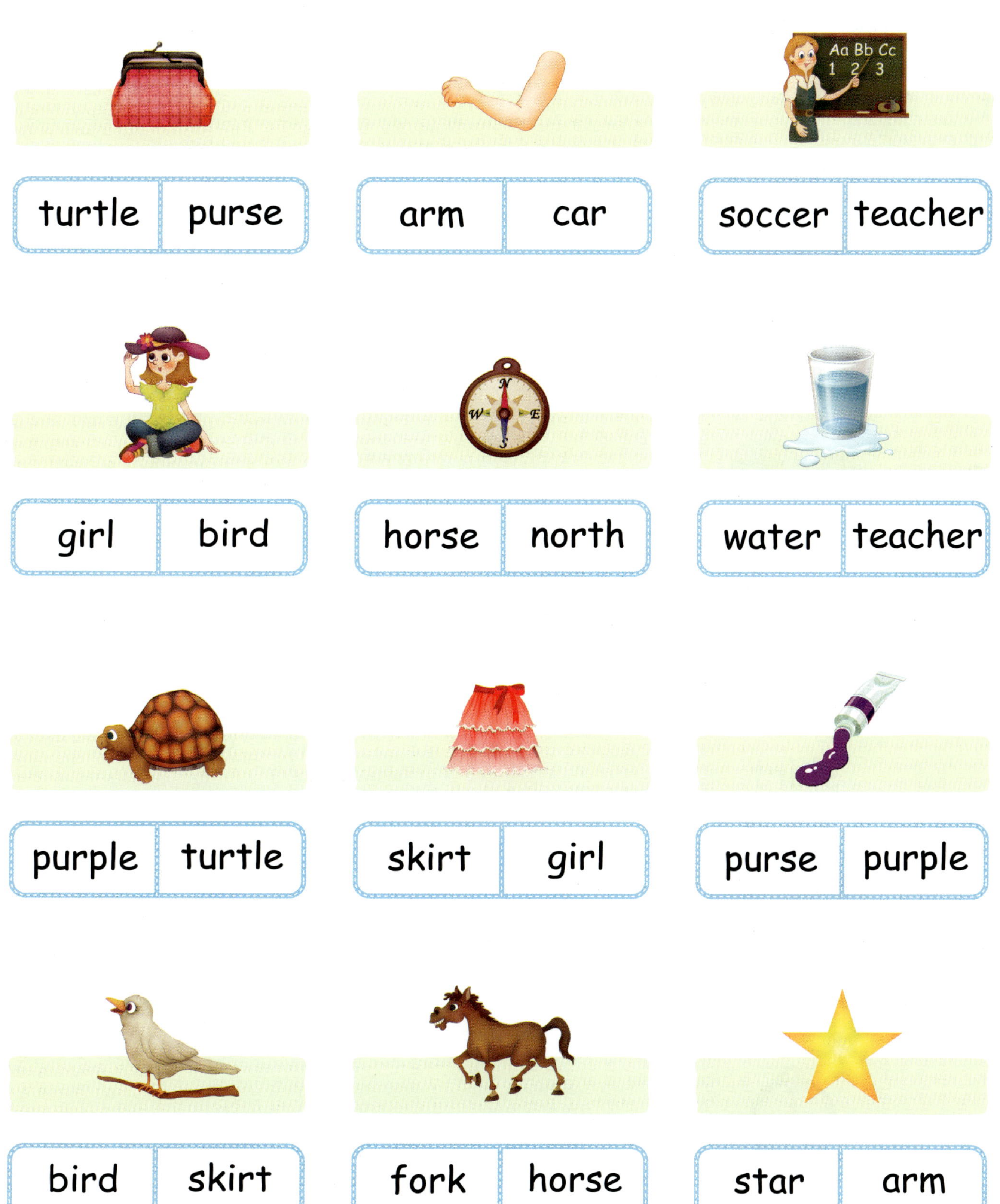

C Write the words with the same double letters.

star	bird	purse	water	fork
purple	teacher	girl	horse	arm

1 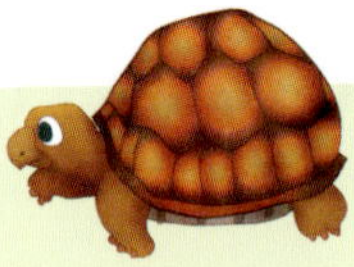

turtle ________ ________

2 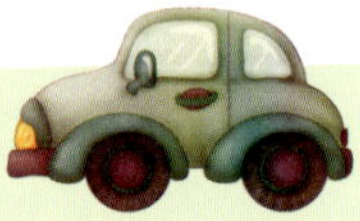

car ________ ________

3 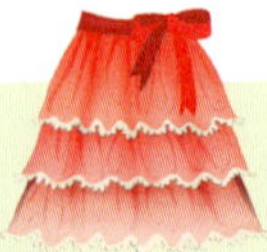

skirt ________ ________

4 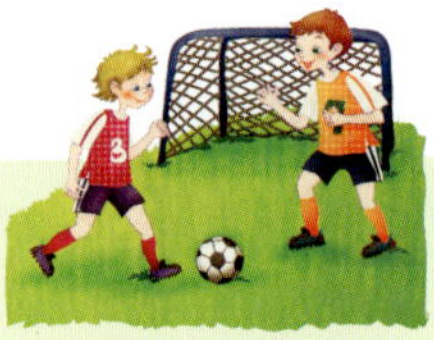

soccer ________ ________

5 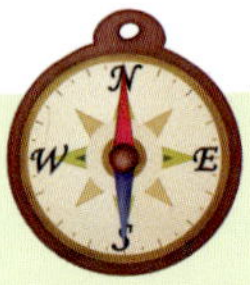

north ________ ________

D Find the words. ↓ → ↘ ↑

purse   arm   bird   water   fork

w	i	e	r	p	o
b	m	b	o	p	s
d	r	j	i	u	v
w	a	t	e	r	y
r	c	e	a	s	d
f	o	r	k	e	g

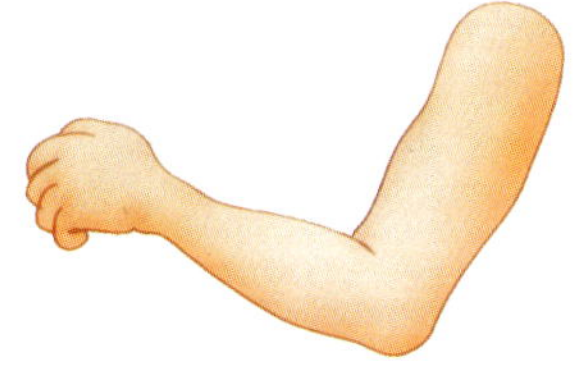

oa ow1 ou ow2

A Fill in the blanks.

c _____

h ____ se

b ___ t

b ___ l

m ___ th

____ l

wind ___

r ___ d

Ⓑ Circle the correct words.

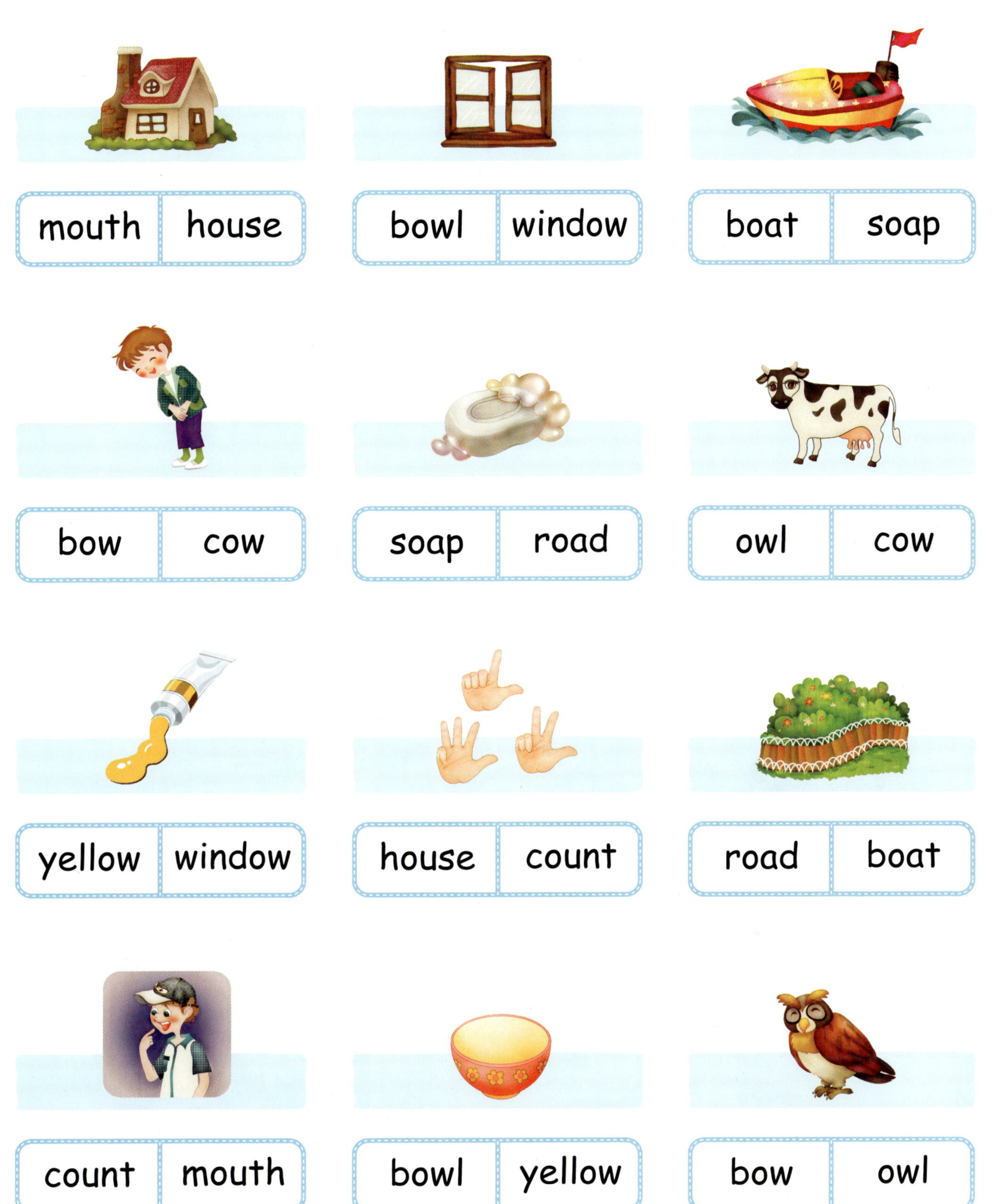

Write the words with the same double letters.

road	owl	mouth	window
yellow	house	cow	boat

1 count

2 bowl

3 bow

4 soap

D **Find the words.** ↓ → ↘ ↑

> cow   boat   mouth   bowl

c	d	s	j	s	c
i	b	m	a	y	o
l	o	o	h	c	w
w	u	n	a	k	u
o	m	o	u	t	h
b	t	r	p	e	x

oi oy oo1 oo2

A Fill in the blanks.

b _____

p __ __ nt

w __ __ d

m __ __ n

t _____

f __ __ d

b __ __ k

c __ __ n

Ⓑ Circle the correct words.

 Write the words with the same double letters.

| food | soil | book | toy |
| coin | moon | wood | oyster |

1 zoo

2 point

3 foot

4  boy

D Find the words. ↓ → ↘ ↑

book   toy   moon   coin

t	q	w	j	a	y
m	r	c	s	y	o
h	o	c	l	v	t
r	b	o	o	k	e
e	s	i	n	g	d
m	o	n	o	t	r

CERTIFICATE

Name

Date

Signed

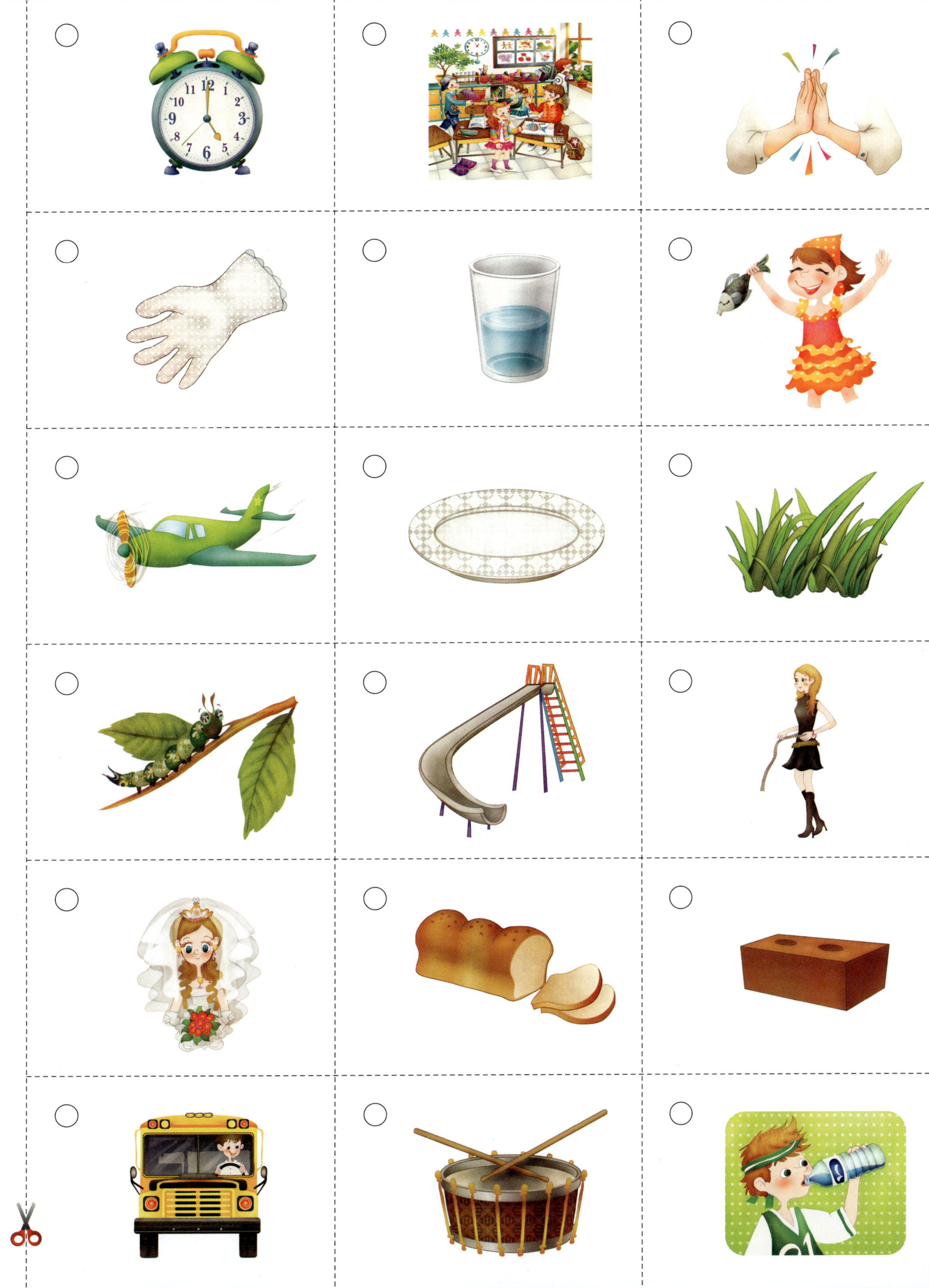

clap	class	clock
glad	glass	glove
plant	plate	plane
slim	slide	slow
brick	bread	bride
drink	drum	drive

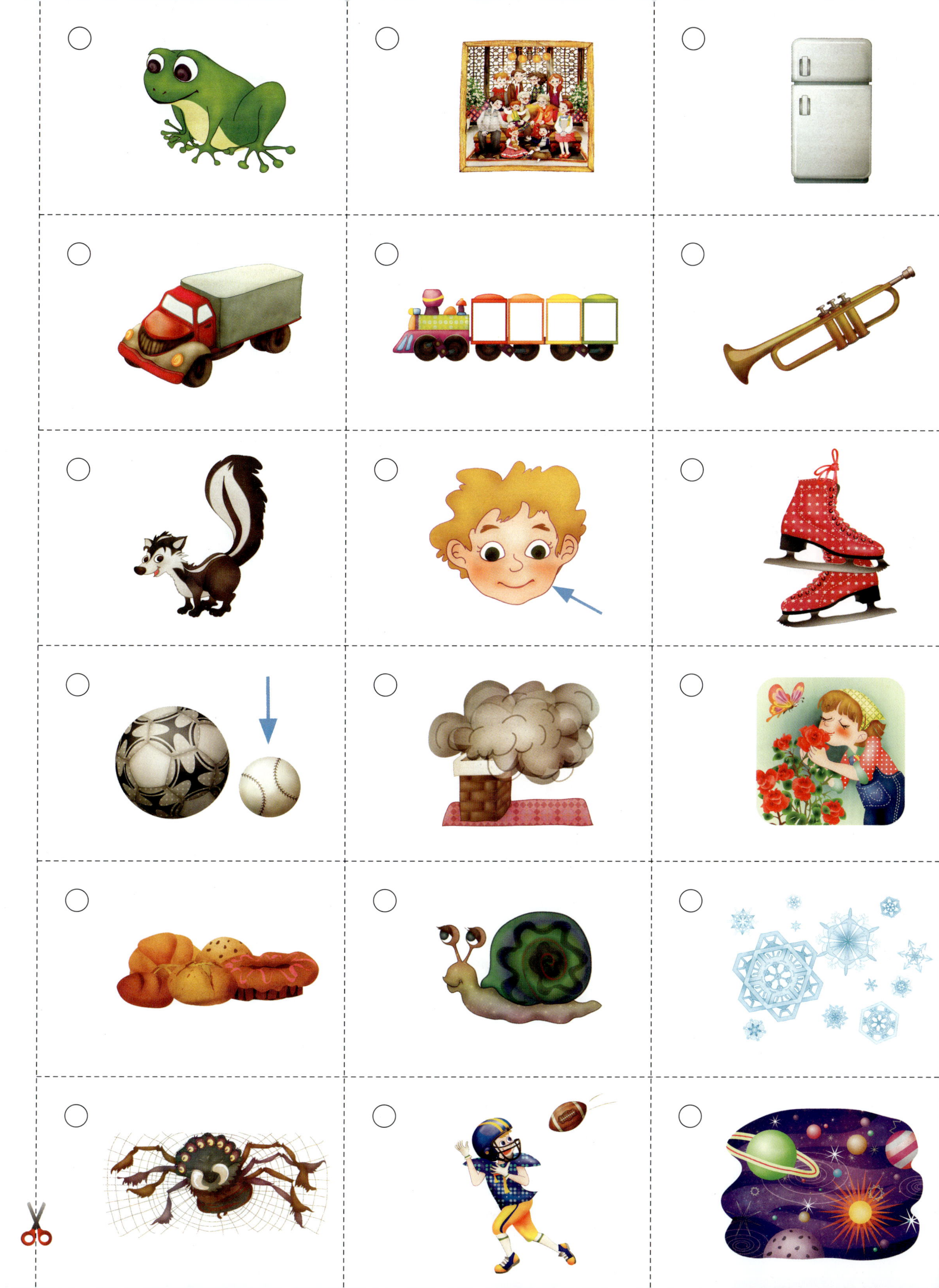

front	frame	frog
trumpet	train	truck
skate	skin	skunk
smell	smoke	small
snow	snail	snack
space	sport	spider

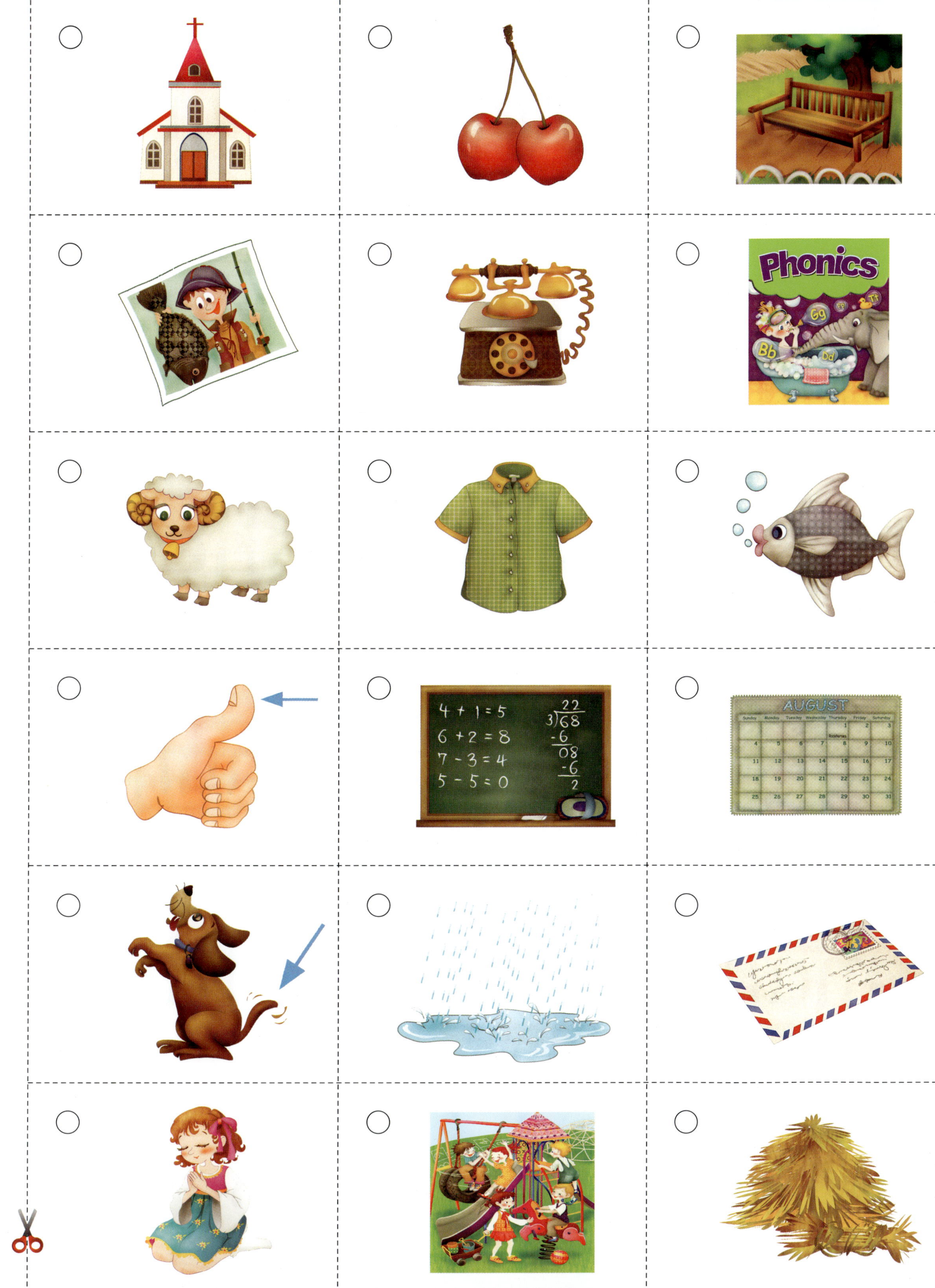

bench	cherry	church
phonics	phone	photo
fish	shirt	sheep
month	math	thumb
mail	rain	tail
hay	play	pray

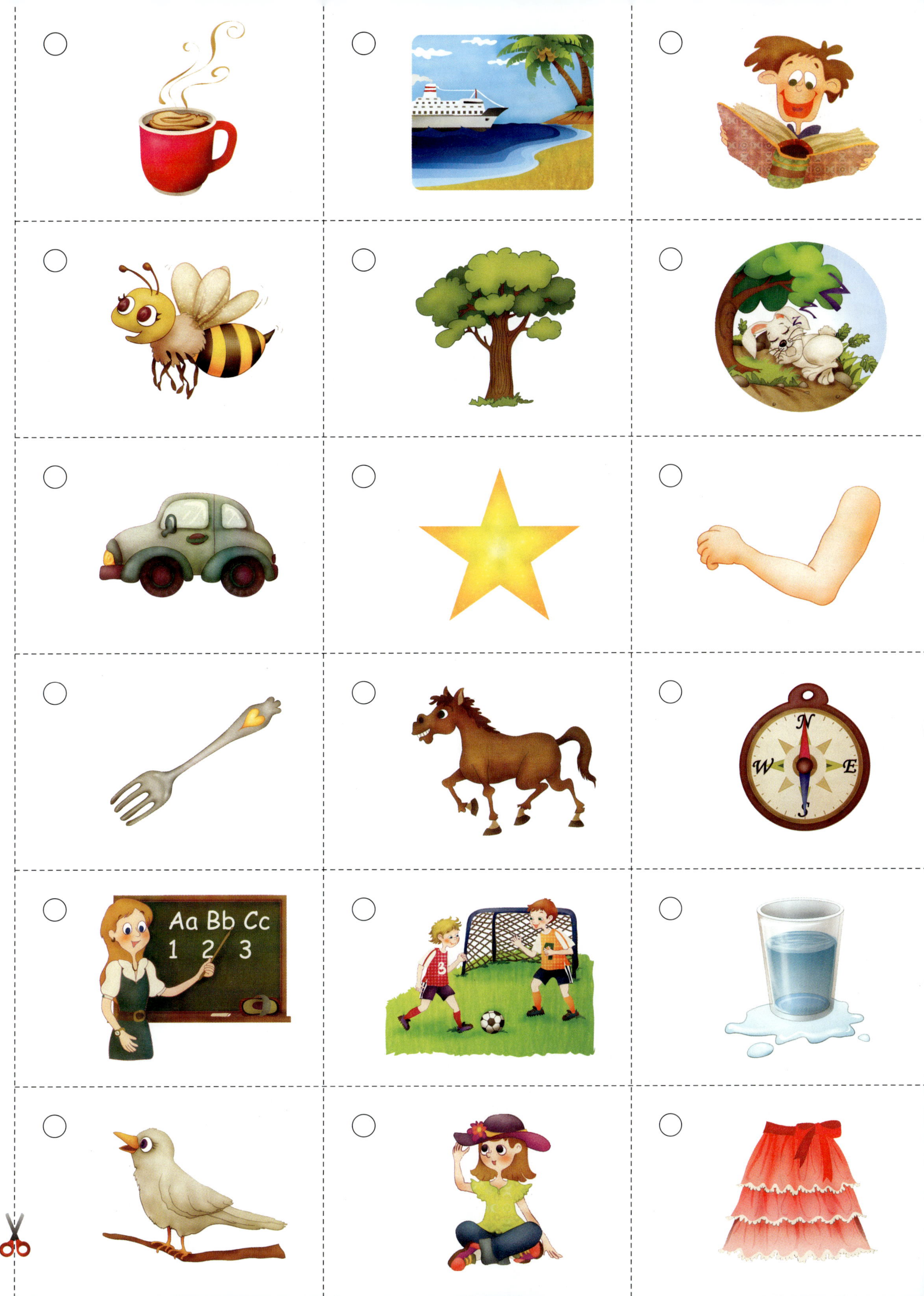

read	sea	tea
sleep	tree	bee
arm	star	car
north	horse	fork
water	soccer	teacher
skirt	girl	bird

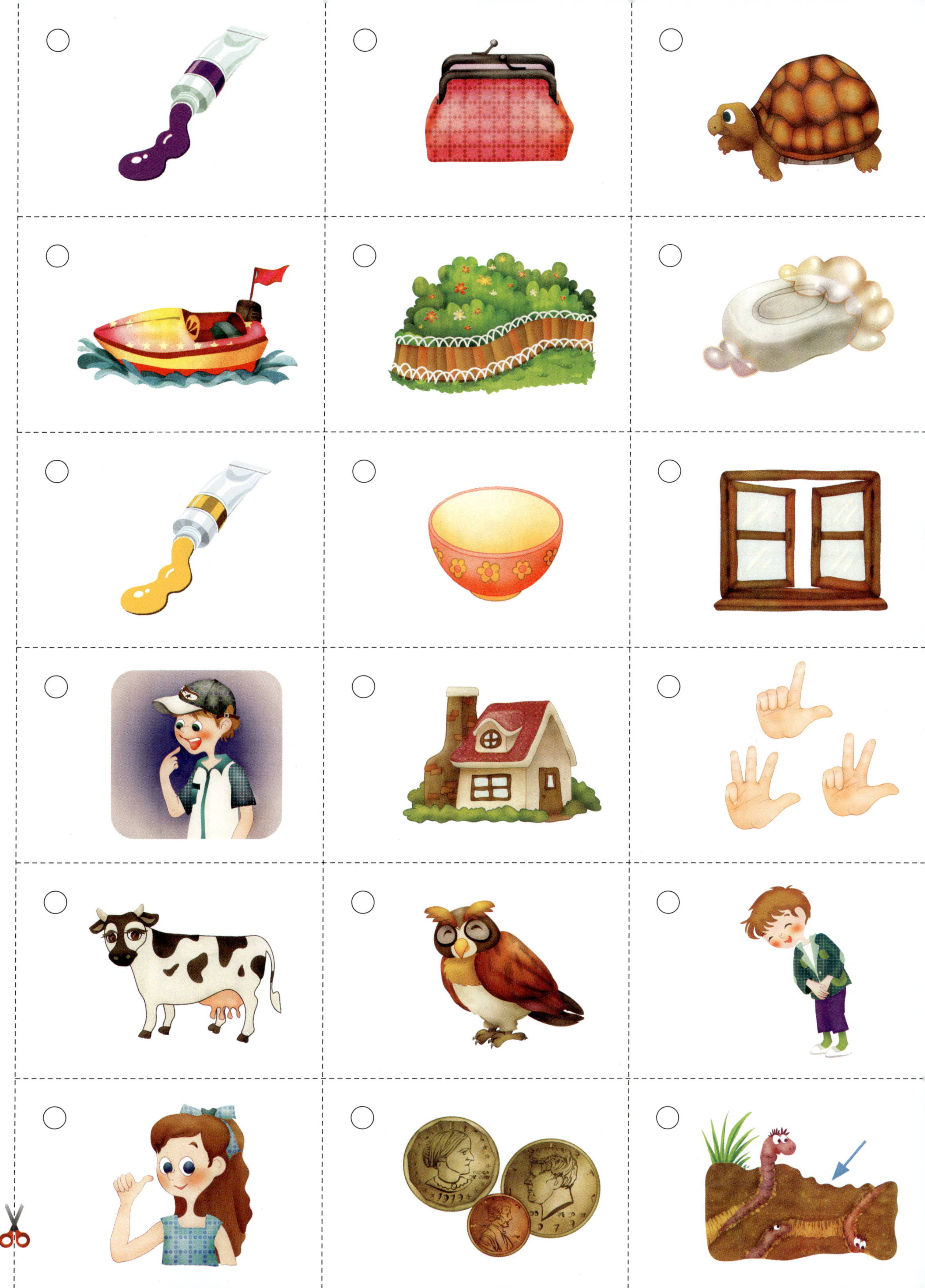

turtle	purse	purple
soap	road	boat
window	bowl	yellow
count	house	mouth
bow	owl	cow
soil	coin	point

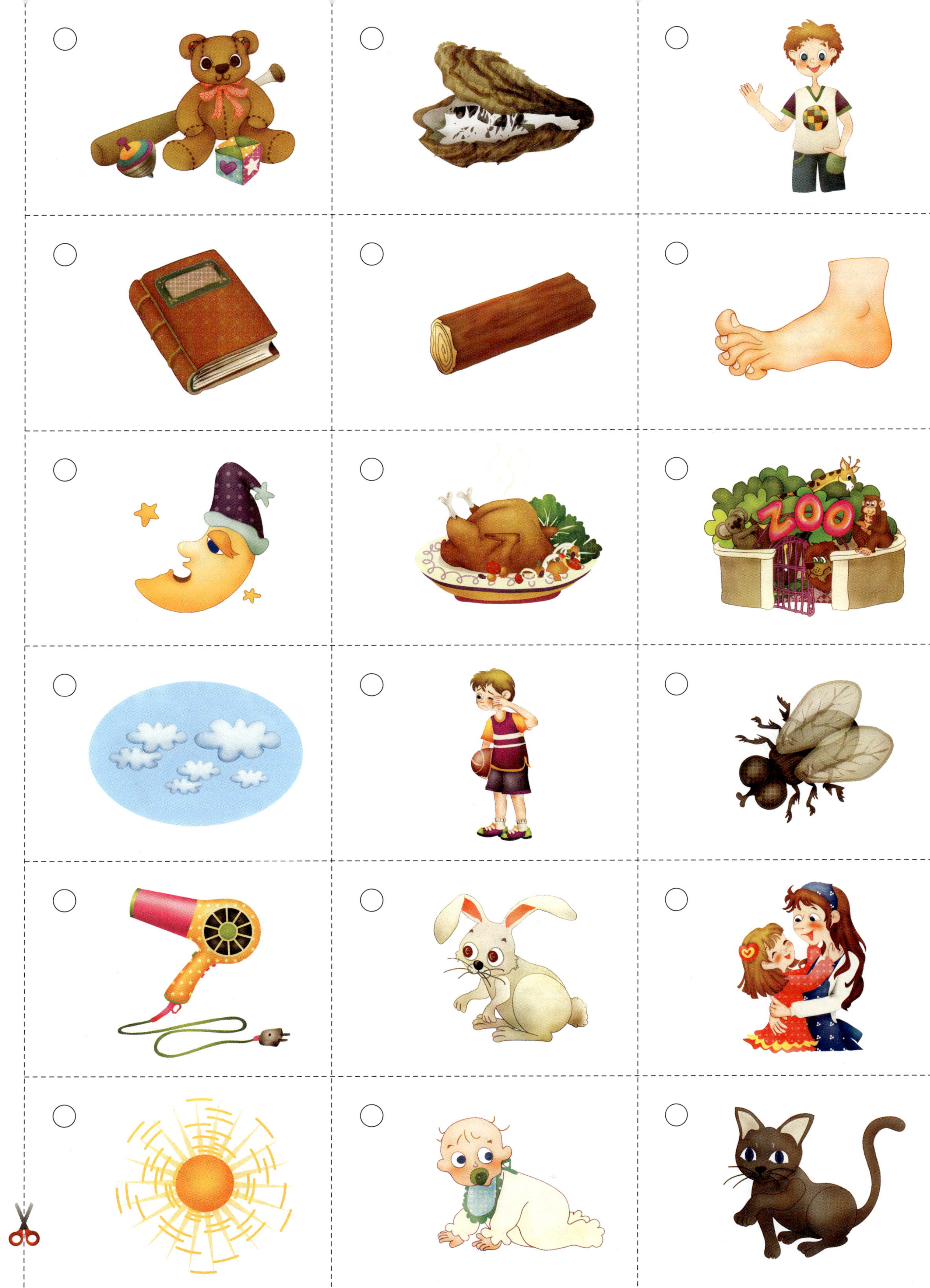

boy	oyster	stoy
foot	wood	book
zoo	food	moon
fly	cry	sky
happy	bunny	dry
cat	baby	sunny

cereal	cone	cup
game	cycle	city
gentle	gum	goat
	gym	giraffe